Glimpses
of
Chinese Culture

掠影 中国历史文化

丁往道 著

外语教学与研究出版社
FOREIGN LANGUAGE TEACHING AND RESEARCH PRESS
北京 BEIJING

图书在版编目（CIP）数据

中国历史文化掠影 = Glimpses of Chinese Culture：英文 / 丁往道
著. —— 北京 ：外语教学与研究出版社，2021.7（2024.8 重印）
ISBN 978-7-5213-2885-1

Ⅰ. ①中… Ⅱ. ①丁… Ⅲ. ①英语－阅读教学－教材②文化史－
中国－英文 Ⅳ. ①H319.37

中国版本图书馆 CIP 数据核字（2021）第 166179 号

出 版 人　王　芳
责任编辑　崔　超　杨　飘
责任校对　张俊睿
封面设计　李　高
版式设计　水长流文化
出版发行　外语教学与研究出版社
社　　址　北京市西三环北路 19 号（100089）
网　　址　https://www.fltrp.com
印　　刷　北京捷迅佳彩印刷有限公司
开　　本　889×1194　1/32
印　　张　7
版　　次　2021 年 9 月第 1 版 2024 年 8 月第 4 次印刷
书　　号　ISBN 978-7-5213-2885-1
定　　价　39.00 元

如有图书采购需求，图书内容或印刷装订等问题，侵权、盗版书籍等线索，请拨打以下电话或
关注官方服务号：
客服电话：400 898 7008
官方服务号：微信搜索并关注公众号"外研社官方服务号"
外研社购书网址：https://fltrp.tmall.com

物料号：328850001

记载人类文明
沟通世界文化
www.fltrp.com

出版说明

全球一体化的趋势，让中国与其他国家的距离越来越近。而随着近年来中外交流日益频繁，越来越多的外国朋友迫切渴望探知中国的文化。为此，我们呈献上这本英文版《中国历史文化掠影》。

本书没有厚重的中国历史，没有繁复的文化全景。它只是用随笔的形式，为读者在悠久漫长的中国历史长河中撷取最为精彩、最为耀眼的片断。

全书语言优美，风格清新。即使在此之前，对中国文化一无所知的人，通过阅读本书也可以很容易地走进中国文化所经历的五千年，从而从古老的历史中读懂今天中国的一点一滴。

本书对于外国朋友来说，是轻松了解中国文化的一条捷径。而本书英语平易流畅，对于希望提高英语水平和翻译能力的大、中学生来说，也不失为一个优秀的读本。

本书第一版为中英双语对照，一经出版便受到广大读者的欢迎。此次邀请作者进行修订，增加了一些新的内容，并增添了相应的图片，以便让读者对中国文化有更为直观的了解。

Preface

The global integration has brought China closer to the rest of the world. With the frequent exchanges between China and other countries in recent years, more and more foreigners are eager to have a better understanding of the culture of China. *Glimpses of Chinese Culture* is designed for this purpose.

Instead of elaborating on the complicated Chinese history and culture, the book, in the form of short essays, describes the most gorgeous episodes in the long history of Chinese culture for readers.

The subjects are presented in a way that is fresh and vivid. Even readers without prior knowledge of Chinese culture will find it easy to delve into China's five-thousand-year history and to understand contemporary China from a historical perspective.

The book provides overseas readers with a shortcut to Chinese culture. Its highly readable language makes itself a good copy for university and high school students who have a desire to improve their English and translation skills.

The first edition of this book comes in both Chinese and English, which has gained popularity among readers. With the new contents and pictures, the present edition will enable readers to have a deeper understanding of Chinese culture.

A Chronological Table of Chinese History

Xia	c.2070–1600 BC
Shang (Yin)	c.1600–1046 BC
Zhou	
Western Zhou	c.1046–771 BC
Eastern Zhou	770–256 BC
Spring and Autumn Period	770–476 BC
Warring States Period	475–221 BC
Qin	221–207 BC
Han	
Western Han	202 BC–AD 8
Eastern Han	25–220
Three Kingdoms	
Wei	220–265
Shu	221–263
Wu	222–280
Jin	
Western Jin	265–316
Eastern Jin	317–420
Sixteen States	304–439
Southern and Northern Dynasties	
Northern Dynasties	386–581
Southern Dynasties	420–589

Sui	581–618
Tang	618–907
Five Dynasties and Ten States	907–979
Song	
Northern Song	960–1127
Southern Song	1127–1276
Liao	916–1125
Western Xia	1038–1227
Jin	1115–1234
Yuan	1271–1368
Ming	1368–1644
Qing	1644–1911
Republic of China	1912–1949
People's Republic of China	Founded in 1949

Contents

01

Beginnings of
Chinese Culture

Portrait of Huangdi

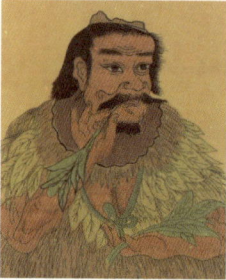
Portrait of Yandi

The Chinese people are proud of their long history.

About 5,000 years ago, Huangdi, the Yellow Emperor, according to legend, ruled part of the Yellow River valley. He and another leader, Yandi, or the Fiery Emperor, made great contributions to the progress of civilization. Huangdi is said to have invented the cart, the boat, the clothes, the script and the medicine, and Yandi to have taught people how to turn the soil with a plow. Today, Chinese regard them as their earliest ancestors, calling themselves "Yan-Huang's descendants."

Many, many years after them, Yao, Shun and Yu led the people one after another. Yu was popular and prestigious, for legend has it that he had tamed the flooding rivers by channelling their waters into the sea. Upon his death, Yu was succeeded by his son Qi. Thus the first dynasty in Chinese history was founded. It was called the Xia. This event marked the change from primitive society, where there was no family, private property, or class distinction, to a class society based on the family and private ownership.

The Xia, which lasted about 400 years, was overthrown by the Shang, a state in the east. The Shang Dynasty was to rule the middle and lower reaches of the Yellow River for about 500 years before it was replaced by the Zhou.

It should be noted that Chinese history before the Shang Dynasty, though recorded in several ancient classics, is mainly legendary. So far no material evidence has been discovered to prove that Huangdi, Yao, Shun, Yu and the Xia Dynasty really existed. However, the existence of the Shang has been proved by the oracle bones and other things unearthed in Anyang, Henan Province, about a century ago. According to recent research, the Xia was founded in about 2070 BC, and the Shang in about 1600 BC.

Oracle bones

The Shang rulers were superstitious. Before they made an important decision, they would ask their court diviners to predict if the occasion was favourable. They would take an ox bone or a tortoise shell, drill a hole in it, and put it over a fire until cracks developed. Then they would study the cracks, from which they could foretell whether the action considered would have good or bad results. Both the conclusion they drew from the cracks and the real result of the action, if it was performed, would be recorded in a few words on the bone or shell. In this way the Shang diviners wrote faithful accounts of many important events of their time.

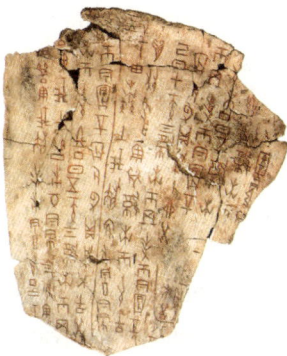

Oracle bone script

Over the years about 100,000 pieces of oracle bones have been discovered and collected in Anyang. The place was certainly one of the capitals, probably the last one, of the Shang which moved its capital several times.

Over 4,000 different words have been found on those bones, indicating that written Chinese was already highly-developed more than 3,000 years ago.

The Shang ruled over a slave society. Slaves, most of whom had been captured in battles with other states or tribes, were forced to till the land and do household work for their masters. What was more tragic was that slaves might be killed as sacrifices to the gods and their masters' ancestors, and might even be buried alive to accompany their masters when they died.

During the 11th century BC, probably in 1046 BC, the Shang Dynasty was conquered by Zhou, a state in the Wei River valley in present-day Shaanxi Province. King Wen of Zhou had made his state strong and planned the conquest. A few years after his death, his son, King Wu, led an army in an attack on the Shang capital and quickly defeated the Shang troops. King Wu became the first king of the new Zhou Dynasty.

Portrait of King Wen

When King Wu died, his sons were still too young to rule the country, so for several years state affairs were directed by King Wu's younger brother, the Duke of Zhou. The political and social systems of the new dynasty were mainly designed by these three founders: King Wen, King Wu and the Duke of Zhou.

Portrait of King Wu

They established a feudal fief system. The whole country was divided into a number of areas, each of which was assigned to a member of the royal family or a noble related by marriage to the rulers, or to the chief of a small state that had been loyal to the Zhou. Not only land, but the people on it, were given to such a man and became his and his descendants' property. This man subdivided his fief into several areas and gave them to members of his family and their descendants. They in turn gave land and people to those under them. It is said that altogether there were six classes in this system, each class having to pay tribute and offer military and other services to the one above.

At the top of this social ladder was the king, the master of all, people and land alike. At the bottom was the serf, bound to the land. He had to work his lord's land before attending to his own small field, and was not allowed to move out of his lord's fief. When there was a war, he had to go and fight. When his lord needed a woman, his wife or daughter might be taken away. In short, his lot was like that of a slave, but was a little better, for he had a small piece of land, a home and a family, and some tools.

The Zhou rulers used two means to maintain law and order: Severe punishments to keep the serfs and common people obedient, and rites to adjust relations among the nobles. The rites were rules of behavior and conduct, regulations of ceremonies and social institutions. The basic principle was that the rites should never apply to the common people and punishments should never apply to the nobles.

These systems and institutions suited the social conditions very well and the Zhou enjoyed peace and stability for about 300 years. Then in 771 BC natural calamities, internal struggles in the court and attacks by border tribes brought Zhou's rule to the brink of collapse. In the following year the capital had to be moved from Haojing in the west to Luoyi, now Luoyang, to its east. From then on the dynasty was called the Eastern Zhou, and the period from 1046 to 771 BC the Western Zhou.

The history of the Eastern Zhou was divided into two periods. The first 300 years, 770–476 BC, was called the Spring and Autumn Period, because all the important events of this period were recorded in a historical work called *The Spring and Autumn Annals*. The period from 475 to 221 BC was called the Warring States Period, because there were continual wars among the states. The dynasty was finally brought to an end in 256 BC, and 35 years later, in 221 BC, China was unified by the Qin Dynasty.

During the Spring and Autumn and Warring States Periods, the king was the ruler and master of the country in name only. He was weak in every way and unable to control the nobles who had large fiefs. The area under his direct rule was becoming smaller and smaller as a result of invasions by nobles who were no longer loyal to him. Powerful states often tried to occupy the land of weaker ones, and they fought each other to increase their influence. As wars went on, the number of states was reduced from over 1,000 during the Western Zhou to about 100 during the Spring and Autumn Period, and to about 20 at the beginning of the Warring States Period.

Portrait of the First Emperor of the Qin

There were great social changes too. The increasing use of iron tools helped to develop agriculture. Landowners came to

realize that they could get more from their
land than the old serf system if it
was turned into plots and rented
to their serfs. Gradually their
"common fields"—fields

Iron tools

formerly tilled by their serfs without pay—became private fields
leased out to their serfs for rent. Thus serf-owners became in
effect landowners and serfs became tenants, who showed greater
interest in production and enjoyed greater independence and
freedom than they had as serfs.

Along with the development of agriculture, handicrafts and
commerce also developed, and there appeared a new merchant
class. Many merchants were rich enough to visit and bribe princes
and dukes.

Another group of people, scholars, also developed. They
came from different classes. Before the Spring and Autumn
Period, what learning there was had been monopolized by the
nobles; they alone could use the books and documents stored by
the government, and other people could not share this right. The
great political and social changes during the Spring and Autumn
and Warring States Periods broke the monopoly of learning by
the nobles. At all levels of society—declining nobles, new
landlords, free citizens, even poor people—there were people
who made an effort to study and turn themselves into scholars.
When rulers of states wanted wise advice that would help them to
make their states rich and strong, they turned to scholars for such
help and often put them to important positions.

The Spring and Autumn and Warring States Periods were
thus a time of change. States expanded or were conquered. The
old systems and institutions established in the Western Zhou were

no longer observed. The rites and original social order were broken. Old beliefs collapsed and new ideas spread. This turbulent situation urged scholars of the day to think of ways to bring about peace and stability, or to make a state rich and strong. Some of them went a step further to study fundamental principles of the universe and human life. Therefore these two periods, especially the Warring States Period, saw the rise of many different schools of philosophy. It was a period when, as people often say, a hundred schools of thought contended.

02

Confucius:
The First Private Teacher
in Chinese History

The first and most important scholar of the Spring and Autumn Period was Confucius. He was born in the state of Lu, in present-day Shandong Province, in 551 BC. His surname was Kong, Qiu was his given name, and Zhongni his courtesy name. According to legend, before his birth his parents had prayed to the god of Mount Niqiu for a son, so they called him Qiu and Zhongni. Confucius is his Latinized name, which has been used in the West ever since he was known abroad.

Confucius was only three years old when his father, a noble man of the lowest rank, died. In Qufu, the capital of Lu, mother and son led a hard life. Young Confucius showed a great interest in study, and his mother did everything possible to encourage him. But she did not live to see her son established as a scholar and died when he was 16 or 17.

Later, recalling his own earlier days, Confucius said, "At 15 I made up my mind to study; at 30 I was established." It appears that he had in his youth studied what classics there were to study and formed his own thoughts and views on the most important problems of history, society and mankind. From then on his main goal was to practice and spread his views, and in so doing to bring light to people who were groping in darkness for the right ways of life.

Confucius teaching at the Apricot Altar

The method he adopted was education. He gave instruction to all who came to learn from him.

By then a well-known scholar, he set up a sort of private school. This was an event of great historic significance. Before Confucius, only the children of the nobles had the right to education, while ordinary people were kept illiterate. Confucius was the first person in Chinese history to bring education to all people, and in particular to those of ordinary birth.

From the age of about 30 to his death at 73, he never stopped teaching. It was said that altogether he taught about 3,000 students, 72 of whom had outstanding achievements in the academic or political field.

His influence increased with the number of his students, and the rulers of Lu came to realize that it might be proper to make him an official in the government. For a few years he helped to govern the state, and his work brought about very good results. But those nobles who had real control of the government did not like his measures; they made it difficult for him to carry out his ideals. So he decided to leave. He was then 55 years old.

Confucius visiting the states

During the next 14 years, accompanied by several faithful students, Confucius visited nine states and talked with the rulers of six of them, trying to convince them of the necessity of humane government, and hoping that his principles would be put into practice. But none of the rulers were interested in his views. As they were all anxious to make their states rich and strong, humane government must have sounded to them too abstract and impractical to adopt.

During his absence, a new generation of nobles had come into power in Lu. At their invitation Confucius returned home, when he was 68 years old. In his last years he did not work in the government, but devoted his time to teaching and editing the classics. In 479 BC, when he was 73, he fell ill and died.

Confucius did not write any books. In his time it was not yet the custom for a man to write for publication. The classics he edited were made up of government documents and historical records handed down from earlier times, and folk songs specially collected over the ages. Moreover, Confucius himself preferred explaining ancient principles to creating new theories.

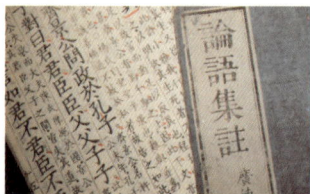

Variorum of the Analects of Confucius

Fortunately there is a book which expresses Confucius's views and theories more directly and clearly than those classics he edited. It is *The Analects of Confucius*, a collection of about 500 sayings of Confucius and his major disciples, and their comments and answers to questions. Obviously they were recorded and compiled by those students who had heard Confucius talking and his disciples discussing the master's teachings. The sayings deal with a wide range of topics: humanity and rites, government and law, education and knowledge, music and poetry, the qualities of gentlemen and the weaknesses of mean men. In addition, there are a few brief descriptions of Confucius' manner, lifestyle and personality. Discussions of Confucius' philosophy are generally based on this valuable book.

Confucius said, "If I learned the Way in the morning, I would die contently in the evening." This saying expresses his love for and eagerness to seek the truth, which is what the Way roughly means. He spent all his life studying, spreading and promoting the Way. To him the Way was life, or the thing he lived for. He put forward a series of theories about man, life, society and government. Together they formed his Way.

As we know, the ruling class of his day was greedy and ambitious, cruel and oppressive. The common people, on the other hand, lived in great misery, bound hand and foot by harsh laws, unjust traditions, and blind faith in Heaven, ghosts and fate. Confucius was determined to save mankind from this tragic condition by means of reasoning. He wanted to awaken all people to a correct understanding of the nature of man and the right way to be a man. For this purpose he stressed the importance of man's moral nature.

"To be humane is to be a man." he said. This saying may mean that humanity or humaneness is the fundamental quality of man, and that it is this quality that makes a man a true man. It may also mean that without this quality a man is not a real man.

As man has a moral nature, to adhere to moral principles should be everyone's first consideration. Moral principles are more important than all other things, including position, wealth, even life. Confucius said, "Wealth and high position are desired by all men, but I would not have them if they were not won in the right way. Poverty and low position are hated by all men, but I would not leave them if they could not be rid of in the right way."

Confucius gave very clear explanations to the meaning of humanity: It means to love other men, to help others to stand up when they want to stand up themselves, and to help others to understand things when they want to understand things themselves, and not to impose on others what they do not desire themselves.

Confucius himself loved other men. At that time when social classes were distinct, he accepted as students people from all levels of society and taught all of them. Yan Hui, for instance, was a poor man, and Confucius gave him more praises than any other students. In teaching his students, Confucius was in fact helping them to stand up (succeed) and understand things (the truth).

Mencius said, "Whenever he saw someone drowning, Yu felt as if he had been the cause; whenever he saw someone hungry, Ji felt as if he had been the cause." He who has this feeling is a humane man.

Humanity is the supreme principle. To realize it, one should if necessary give up everything else, including life itself. Confucius said, "A determined or humane man never gives up humanity to save his life, but he may sacrifice his life to realize humanity."

In connection with humanity, Confucius mentioned many other virtues, such as rightness, propriety, wisdom, trustworthiness, loyalty, forbearance, filial piety and brotherly love. He called a man who had virtues a gentleman and a man who was not virtuous a mean man. A virtuous man is always open and sincere, ready to help other men,

Portrait of Yan Hui

free from worries and fears, and at peace with himself and the world. He was describing such a man when he praised Yan Hui, "Hui is a perfect man! No one else could bear his hardships— living in a poor hut with only a bowl of food and a gourd of water—but he is happy. Hui is a perfect man!"

As to the way to govern a state, Confucius urged rule by virtue and humane government. He was against the use of harsh laws and severe punishments, which were common in those days. Repressive measures, according to him, would only make the common people try hard to avoid punishments, and would not help them to distinguish between right and wrong or give them a sense of shame. He held that the ruler himself should be an upright man, and should guide the common people with virtue, and regulate their conduct and behavior with the rites, which were standards of behavior laid down by the rulers of the Western Zhou. He also urged putting only virtuous and talented people to government positions.

What humane government means is made clear in one of his talks with his students: Confucius was in the state of Wei, and Ran You was driving him. Confucius said, "What a dense population!" Ran You said, "When the population is dense, what should be done then?" "Make them rich." "When they are rich, what should be done then?" "Educate them."

So the people should be made rich first and then educated. This should be a good principle even today, for it covers both material and spiritual civilization. They have to be developed at the same time to ensure the stability of the state and the happiness of the people. What great wisdom is shown in this political view!

Confucius was China's first educator, and no doubt one of the world's first educators. As a teacher in all his adult life, he not only set up a school, but also developed significant educational principles and methods of teaching.

"I teach everyone without making distinctions." he said. This was really an epoch-making declaration, for it was an open rebellion against the tradition that education was for the nobles only. By bringing education to the common people he made an immeasurable contribution to the development of Chinese culture.

To Confucius all men were educable because men had a similar nature. "By nature men are pretty alike," he said, "but

Confucius giving a lecture

learning and practice set them apart." This statement, which opposed the common view of his day that the nobles were born superior to the common people, expressed his belief in equality.

Confucius had a clear aim in educating his students: He expected them to be virtuous, to understand man and society, to have a good knowledge of the past and a clear vision of the future, and to devote themselves to the spreading and carrying out of the Way. He did not wish them to become experts in particular fields. So when one of his students asked to be taught how to grow crops, he criticized the student and called him a "mean man." This dislike of specific skills was of course not helpful to the development of science in China.

Confucius' main teaching method was conversation, or question and answer. Sometimes a student would come to him with a question, and he would give him a clear answer. Sometimes a student would express a view, and the master would comment on it. Sometimes the master would start a conversation with a student to explain a theory to him, or direct his attention to a question, or point out the way forward for him. Occasionally the master might talk with more than two students at the same time. *The Analects* is full of records of such conversations.

In his conversations with his students, Confucius often commented on real events and people, and took into consideration the needs of the listener. He might give different answers to the same question asked by different students. He encouraged his students to learn and think, and warned them not to learn without thinking or think without learning. He said, "He who learns without thinking will be bewildered; he who thinks without learning will be in danger."

Confucius and his students had very close relationship. They were united on the basis of the Way, to achieve which was their common goal. For this reason, Confucius cared for and loved his students, always ready to answer their questions and give them the guidance they needed. His students, in return, were loyal and respectful to him; some of them accompanied him on his journey through the states, sharing with him all the difficulties and dangers. One entry in *The Analects* says, "When Confucius was detained in Kuang, Yan Hui was the last to join him. Confucius said, 'I thought you had died.' Yan Hui said, 'As you are alive, how dare I die?'" Yan Hui's words are very moving. He expressed the feeling that he would always follow his teacher, to the point of living and dying with him. It is only natural that this teacher-student relationship should be taken as a model in later ages.

Confucius' views on the mean, on harmony, and on knowledge and practice also had a great influence on the thinking of the Chinese people.

In 134 BC Emperor Wu of the Han Dynasty decided to make Confucianism the state thought. From then on, except a few short periods like the Wei and Jin dynasties, Confucianism was the mainstream of Chinese thought for about 2,000 years. Its influence was most extensive and penetrating.

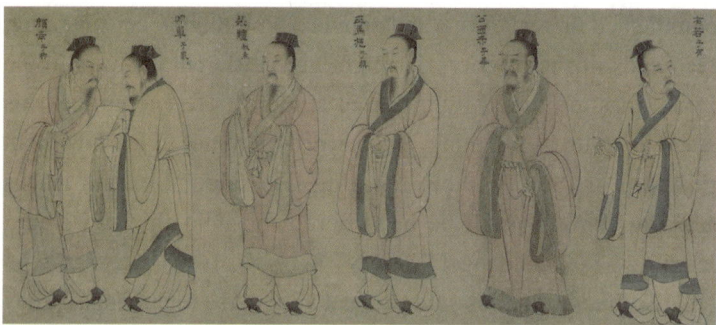

Portrait of Disciples of Confucius (part), by Yan Liben of the Tang Dynasty

03

Lao Zi:
The Founder of Taoism

Confucianism was, as we have mentioned, the mainstream of Chinese thought for about 2,000 years, from the second century BC down to the beginning of the 20th century. The second greatest influence on Chinese thought was no doubt Taoism, which opposed but complemented and enlivened Confucianism.

Portrait of Lao Zi

We know very little about Lao Zi, the founder of Taoism. According to the *Records of the Grand Historian* by Sima Qian, he was born in the State of Chen, in present-day Henan Province, a little earlier than Confucius. He worked for some time in the Zhou government. When he saw the decline of the dynasty, he left his work to live in seclusion. On his way he reached a gate which he had to go through. The gate keeper by the name of Yin Xi begged him to write a book. Lao Zi agreed and wrote about 5,000 words on *dao* and *de*, or the Way and its functions. After that he left and no one knew where he was or when he died.

There have been scholars who hold that Lao Zi may have lived in the 6th century BC, but the book named after him contains ideas and terms that belonged to a much later period. Like many other Chinese classics, the book went through a process of editing and compilation, and may have taken the present shape in the 4th century BC, in the middle of the Warring States Period.

The book is written in verse, in very terse language, with many lines capable of different interpretations. Countless notes to and commentaries on the book have been written by scholars of the past and present. It has been translated into many foreign languages and modern Chinese.

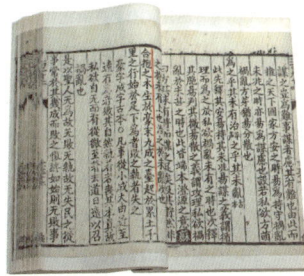

Dao De Jing

Indeed, few books have attracted as much attention and aroused as much interest in China and abroad as this small book.

As it discusses *dao* and *de*, the book is called the *Dao De Jing*, but more commonly known as the *Lao Zi*. The philosophy explained in it is called *Taoism*, for *Tao*, not *Dao*, was how the Chinese word was represented in English in the past.

Dao, according to Lao Zi, gave birth to the universe and make all the things in the universe what they are. In other words, it is the origin of all things, and also the law that governs their workings and change. It is invisible, intangible, and indescribable. In fact, it is nameless, and *Dao* is only an inadequate name forced upon it.

As to the law that governs the development and change of all the things in the universe, Lao Zi put forward a series of profound views. He holds that things and concepts are relative: being and nonbeing produce each other, the difficult and the easy complement each other, the long and the short shape each other, the high and the low contain each other, and what is before and what is after follow each other. He says when the world recognizes the beautiful as beautiful, there is the ugly; when the world recognizes the good as good, there is the bad (or the evil).

Of every pair of opposite concepts, one produces the other, or the existence of one depends on the existence of the other.

This theory is not difficult to understand. Perhaps we do not know it as a philosophy, but we apply it in our everyday life. When we say someone is tall, for instance, we mean that he is taller than many other people, or we know that many other people are shorter than he is. We understand that tallness and shortness are relative.

From this relativity, Lao Zi goes on to draw a very important conclusion, "Reversion is the movement of *Dao*," or turning back is how the Way moves. This means that a state or quality has its process of development, and when it reaches the extreme, it will eventually turn back to its opposite state or quality. In nature and in human society countless examples can be found to prove this theory. Plants, animals, and human beings grow and grow, but one day they will die and disappear. In China and in other countries, there were in the past big, powerful states led by great leaders or conquerors, but all of them collapsed or fell after a period of time.

Lao Zi says that an army that is strong will be defeated, just as a tree that is strong will be broken. This is perhaps because a strong army is often proud and looks down upon other armies, and sooner or later it will be defeated by the joint forces of the armies it has attacked. A tree that is strong is fragile and can easily be broken in a strong wind; while a weak tree is supple, it bends with the wind but will not be broken. The conclusion drawn from this by Lao Zi is that the soft and weak will overcome the hard and strong, and that "weakness is the function of *Dao*."

Lao Zi also discusses the right way to live, behave and handle things. He advises people to be peaceful, quiet, submissive, tolerant, modest, contented, humble, to live a simple life, not to strive for wealth, fame or power, which will only give one worries and trouble. Even when one has won a great success, one had better withdraw from the scene without claiming credit for it. He says, "He does not show himself, and so is conspicuous; he does not consider himself right, and so is famous; he does not brag, and so is given credit; he is not conceited, and so can endure for long. It is just because he does not contend that no one in the world can contend with him." He also says, "To yield is to be preserved; to bend is to become straight; to be low is to be full; to be worn out is to be renewed; to have little is to gain; to have plenty is to be perplexed."

These sayings also show the truth that a state or quality will turn to its opposite when it reaches the extreme. Another similar saying, which is widely known, is that "good fortune may exist beside misfortune, and misfortune may hide in good fortune." The well-known

Mount Laojun, a sacred Taoist mountain

story about the old man on the frontier losing his horse may be considered a good illustration of this statement. When one of his horses runs away, he says that may be a blessing. Soon the horse comes back, bringing with it another horse. But the old man fears a misfortune may happen. His son, who likes riding a horse, falls from the new horse and breaks his leg. This turns out to be a blessing when a war breaks out, for the son, now crippled, is not called up to fight in the war.

About government and social order, Lao Zi is for *wuwei* (nonaction). It does not mean inactivity, but taking no action that is not natural, that is against the original nature and wishes of the people. It means letting people and society take their own course without being taught or directed. Lao Zi believes that a state is poorly governed when the ruler does too much. He says, "The more prohibitions there are in the world, the poorer the people will be; the more sharp weapons the people have, the more troubled the state will be; the more skills man possesses, the more strange things will appear; the more laws and orders are made, the more thieves and robbers there will be." On the other hand, "if the ruler takes no action, the people will be transformed of themselves; if he loves tranquillity, the people will become correct of themselves; if he engages in no activity, the people will become prosperous of themselves; if he has no desire, the people will become simple of themselves."

Core of Taoism: Yin-yang and the eight trigrams

Lao Zi lived in the turbulent years of the Spring and Autumn Period, when wars, usurpations and intrigues were common. What he wrote about nonaction may have expressed his hatred of the rulers of his day, but at the same time he put forward a very important political view. Many centuries later there was in the West a similar theory: The best government is the one that governs least.

"*Dao* invariably takes no action, and yet there is nothing left undone." Lao Zi says.

The above four aspects, the origin of the universe, the workings of all the things in the universe, the right way to live and behave, and the right way to govern a state, are among the most important questions discussed in the book, the *Lao Zi*.

It is clear that Taoism and Confucianism are different in many ways. Confucius holds that moral principles and moral qualities are most important, and all social ills result from the low moral standard of the ruler and people. A ruler should first of all have a good moral character himself and then try to educate the people and make them virtuous. Only in this way can a state be well governed. But Lao Zi hates to talk about virtues and is against education. In his view, knowledge and wisdom, humaneness and rightness, should all be thrown away, so as to keep people's thinking simple and primitive. In his view, knowledge and wisdom produce evil ideas and make people think of and do bad things. It is therefore the duty of a good ruler to make his people have no knowledge or desire.

Confucius took the Western Zhou as a time with the ideal social and political systems, which he wished to restore. Lao Zi's ideal time is a primitive one: In it people do not use written language, do not use ships, carts, or weapons, and live in very small states; the sound of dogs barking and cocks crowing in one state can be heard in another, but the people of one state will grow old and die without having had any contact with those of another.

Confucius hopes that society will be peaceful and orderly as a result of the conscious effort of the ruler and the people, both of whom value moral principles and knowledge. Lao Zi also dreams of a peaceful and orderly society, but that is possible only when the people return to a primitive simplicity, while the ruler does nothing to meddle in their natural way of life. Perhaps Confucius is realistic, while Lao Zi is romantic.

Over the ages Lao Zi's influence was clear on many scholars, poets, artists, even government officials. Tao Qian, for instance, would rather return to his village to lead the life of a farmer than serve as an official. One of his poems says, "I was in a cage for a long time, but now I have returned to nature."

The famous poet Li Bai wrote many poems in praise of nature and freedom. One of them says, "When I am asked why I want to stay in this mountain, I smile and give no answer. My heart is at peace at seeing peach flowers flowing away with the water, for this is a land different from the world of men."

Taoist influence on traditional Chinese painting can easily be seen. Most landscapes represent beautiful and quiet scenery with mountains and lakes, rocks and trees. There may be no men in them; if there are, they are very small and inconspicuous. They seem to be part of nature or merge with it.

Taoist principles are often followed in garden designing. In a typical Chinese garden there is no straight road or a big central hall. Instead, there are winding paths between bamboos and trees, small houses hidden behind hills or rocks, and ponds with wooden bridges across them. The purpose is to mirror nature and make one feel that he is living in the midst of nature, far from the busy world.

04

The Warring States Period: The Contention of a Hundred Schools

The Warring States Period, which lasted about 250 years, was marked by important social and political changes. Wars and annexations greatly reduced the number of states. Among those left there were seven big powers, which were constantly trying to win hegemony either by plotting or by fighting. In order to increase their economic and military strength, some of the states started reforms. The most effective reform was carried out by Shang Yang in the state of Qin. It was effective because it suited the new social conditions brought about by the transition from a slave to a feudal society.

Along with the social and political changes there arose important philosophers and profound philosophical theories. Schools of thought appeared one after another. Each school had its main theorist and followers. They wrote books to propagate their views and criticize their opponents' fallacies. Later people called this phenomenon the "contention of a hundred schools" though in fact there were not so many contending schools of thought.

One school was led by Mo Di, commonly called Mo Zi. He probably lived between 480 and 420 BC. A craftsman in his youth, he later became a scholar. He first studied Confucianism but then opposed it. Many modern historians have high opinions of him, saying that he spoke for the interests of the working people of his time. Like Confucius he travelled over long distances to visit the rulers of different states, trying in vain to persuade them to into adopting his political principles.

Among his important views were: using virtuous men as officials, unifying thought, practising economy, simplifying funerals, discarding music and other enjoyments, denouncing fatalism, opposing aggression, and practising universal love. The

Portrait of Mo Zi

best-known of these was the theory of universal love. He said that one should regard other states as one's own, other families as one's own, and other people's bodies as one's own. If the rulers of states loved one another, there would be no fighting; if the heads of families loved one another, there would be no seizure of property; if people loved one another, there would be no attacks. If all the people in the world loved one another, the strong would not oppress the weak, the majority would not bully the minority, the rich would not insult the poor, the honored would not despise the humble, and the cunning would not deceive the simple-minded. Universal love would prevent all hatred, calamities, and hostilities.

Meng Ke, also known as Meng Zi or Mencius, was born in Zou in the state of Lu. His family was poor when he was young. It was said that his mother moved house three times so that her son could live in a good neighbourhood. He was taught by one of Zisi's disciples, Zisi being Confucius' grandson. After he became a well-known scholar, he, too, went to many states to talk with their rulers about the right way of

Portrait of Mencius

government. His views were respected, but not adopted. In his old age, he wrote *The Book of Mencius* with the help of some of his disciples.

In his political theory he upheld Confucius' principles of rule by virtue and humane government. He said that a benevolent ruler certainly had the people's support, while a ruthless ruler was hated and would eventually be overthrown by the people. One of his famous sayings was "The people are the most venerable; next come the gods of land and crops; and the king is the least important." This saying contains some democratic spirit.

He held that only those who are morally good can be good rulers or officials. Four moral qualities are the most important: humanity, rightness, propriety and wisdom. These qualities are inherent in man, for they are endowed by Heaven. Everyone has the feeling of sympathy and commiseration, the feeling of shame and resentment, the feeling of respect and modesty, and the feeling of right and wrong. From these feelings grow the above four qualities.

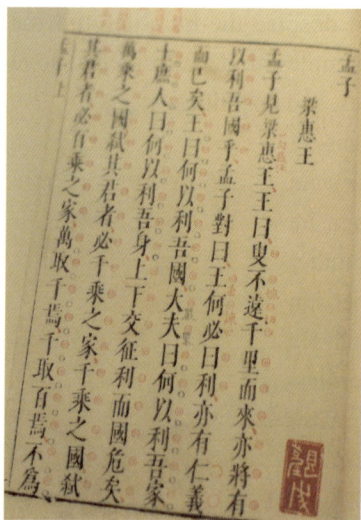

The Book of Mencius

As there are these inborn feelings, human nature is good. But some people are degenerate, even evil, because their good qualities have been obscured by material longings. This possibility shows the necessity of self-cultivation and self-discipline.

In short, Mencius upheld Confucius' principles and in some ways developed Confucianism. Many later rulers and scholars respected him and called him the "Second Sage," second only to Confucius.

Zhuang Zi, whose name was Zhuang Zhou, was born in eastern Henan. His dates are not certain (about 369–286 BC), and little is known about his life. According to the *Zhuang Zi*, the book he is believed to have written, he was poor all his life, sometimes trying to earn a living by making straw sandals,

Portrait of Zhuang Zi

and he was never an important official. Once the king of Chu, who had heard about his learning and personality, sent a man to him with the message that the king wished to use him as the prime minister. Zhuang Zi refused. He said that an ox which was to be used as a sacrifice was well fed, but would be killed when the day came. He preferred to live like a fish in muddy water and enjoy himself.

Zhuang Zi inherited and developed Lao Zi's philosophy. Like Lao Zi, he regarded nonaction as the best way of government. In primitive times, he said, people grew crops and wove cloth, and were not divided into groups or classes. They did not talk about virtues like humanity, rightness, propriety or wisdom. They were not interested in fame or wealth. They lived a free and happy life—a life in agreement with man's nature. He said that the minister who had killed a ruler and taken over his power would invariably call himself a humane man. So names of virtues could be used as a shield by evil doers to protect themselves. In this way he exposed the hypocrisy of the ruling class. He wanted to do away with all political and social systems and go back to the primitive age.

He agreed with Lao Zi that *Tao* gave birth to the universe

and the myriad things in the universe. *Tao* was a formless material and might be called *wu* (nonbeing), but it produced all the things with forms. *Tao* was also *qi* (air), which integrated and became concrete things. When concrete things disintegrated, they returned to *qi*. This also applied to human beings. When a person died, he or she returned to *qi*. It was nothing to be sad about. Death was even a blessing, for it meant peace and freedom. When Zhuang Zi's wife died, he sang to show his congratulations.

He said that man should live a life that suited his original nature. If he could get rid of desires for fame, wealth, and position, he would be able to have peace, freedom and leisure. Things that are natural are good, and things that are artificial are bad. An ideal person is one who is entirely at one with nature, accepts whatever happens to him, has no goal, and makes no conscious effort to achieve anything.

Those who had carried out reforms including Shang Yang were generally called the Legalists. They had an entirely different understanding of the social and political problems facing the states and offered very different solutions. Instead of preaching moral principles, nonaction or universal love, they stressed the necessity of making and enforcing laws. In addition, they held that authority and the method of using men were also important factors in effective government. These views were forcefully explained in the writing of Han Fei (about 280–233 BC), the synthesizer of Legalist theories.

Han Fei was born into a noble family in the state of Han. Seeing the weakness of his state, he wrote many letters to the king, suggesting ways to make it strong, but the king ignored them. Then he devoted his time to writing a book expressing his views. It was called *Han Fei Zi*. The king of Qin, who later unified

China, happened to read the book, and admired the writer's learning and ideas. The king forced Han to send Han Fei to Qin. But, after he arrived in Qin, he was first thrown into prison and then poisoned to death by Li Si, Qin's chief minister. Li Si had once studied with Han Fei under the guidance of Xun Qing, a famous scholar, and knew he was not equal to Han Fei.

According to Han Fei, laws should be made public to all people and should be strictly enforced. Anyone who did anything good according to law should be rewarded, even if he was a common man; anyone who did anything against the law should be punished, even if he was a high-ranking minister. This was a progressive idea at that time, because the privileges of the nobility were not taken into account.

Portrait of Han Fei

The theory behind the view of rule by law was his teacher Xun Qing's assertion that human nature was evil. To Han Fei, relations between men were determined by nothing but personal gains and losses. He said that a carriage maker would wish many people were rich so that they could buy his products, while a coffin maker would wish many people were dying and had to buy his products. It was useless to talk to the common people about humanity and rightness. To make them law-abiding and obedient the ruler had to use severe punishment. Qin followed this theory and made many harsh laws to control the people. But this policy, when pushed to the extreme, would lead to resistance and rebellion. That was why in later dynasties no ruler openly advocated Legalism.

Han Fei held that society was always advancing, and would never go backward. In primitive times, people lived on trees to escape from wild animals and got fire by drilling into wood. If anyone lived like that today, he would be laughed at by all people. He told interesting fables like "Waiting for a Rabbit by the Tree" to ridicule those people who believed that the past was better than the present.

He saw the connection between material wealth and population. If population grew faster than material wealth, there might be social disorder. This was a new theory in his day.

The term *maodun* (contradiction) originated in one of his fables. A man selling spears and shields boasted that his spears were so sharp that they could pierce everything, and that his shields were so strong that nothing could go through them. A spectator then asked him what would happen if one of his spears was used against one of his shields, and the man could not answer. Han Fei said that contradiction was present everywhere, and the two sides of a contradiction were changeable—good fortune might change into misfortune, prosperity into decline, strength into weakness, etc.

Besides the Confucian, Taoist, Moist and Legalist schools that have been mentioned, there were also the Yin-Yang school, the school of Names or Logicians, the school of Vertical and Horizontal Alliance, the school of Strategists, the school of Agriculturalists, and others. Viewed from the angle of political successes in the Warring States Period, the Legalists may be said to have won the contention of the hundred schools. For the state of Qin, which adopted Legalist policies, conquered the other states and unified China. However, in the Western Han that followed the Qin, Confucianism, not Legalism, was made the orthodox thought and was to be the dominant influence on Chinese thought and culture for about 2,000 years.

05

Ancient Historians:
Uninterrupted Recording
of Chinese History

In China the recording of historical events began as far back as over 3,000 years ago, and has never been interrupted. This long, continuous tradition of historical documentation is unique in the world.

In no other country was the writing and study of history so valued as in ancient China. The Chinese people thought that history not only provided information of the past, but also gave moral and political education to future generations.

It has been mentioned that the Shang rulers often ordered their court diviners to foretell, with the help of tortoise shells and ox bones, whether the actions to be taken would be auspicious, and that the diviners would carve a few words on the shells or bones recording the real results of the actions after they were carried out. In this way they made brief but faithful records of many important

Bones with divination inscriptions

events that had happened. Those court diviners could be called the earliest historians in ancient China, though they did not write anything consecutive.

In the Zhou that followed the Shang, there were officials in the government whose main duty was to keep records of important things that happened in the court or in the country, and of unusual natural phenomena. Not only in the king's court, but also in the houses of princes who ruled the states, were there such official historians, who were invariably learned and upright scholars. Their records, when put together, would make up chronicles. In many states those chronicles were called *Spring and Autumn Annals*, perhaps because important events often happened in these two seasons.

One story shows how official historians true to their duties did their work. In 548 BC, in the state of Qi, a powerful minister by the name of Cui Zhu killed the ruler Duke Zhuang. The official historian of the state wrote in the chronicle "Cui Zhu murdered the prince." On reading the entry, Cui Zhu was so angry that he put the historian to death. This man's younger brother, who succeeded him as the official historian, wrote exactly the same words, and was also killed. Then another younger brother was given the job, and he still wrote those words. This time Cui Zhu knew that he could not change the historian's way of making truthful records, so he set free the third brother.

It was said that Confucius believed historical facts, if properly explained, would be more instructive and easier to understand than abstract theories. So he revised and edited the chronicle of the state of Lu, where he was born. It was the *Spring and Autumn Annals* that gave the 242 years (722–481 BC) it covered a name: the Spring and Autumn Period. Its system of recording events according to the sequence of time was a great invention in the way of writing histories. The facts entered into his chronicle was generally accurate. For instance, more than 30 of the eclipses mentioned in it have been confirmed by modern scientists.

In editing the book, Confucius was careful with the choice of words. The laudatory and derogatory words he used showed his approval or condemnation of persons and actions. So Mencius said, "After Confucius completed the *Spring and Autumn Annals*, disloyal ministers and villainous people were in constant fear."

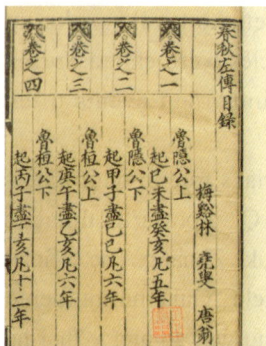

Master Zuo's Spring and Autumn Annals

They were in fear because they knew that their wrong behavior would be condemned as similar behavior had been by Confucius.

As events are only briefly mentioned in this book, there were historians who elaborated on the entries by writing commentaries on them. Those written by Zuo Qiuming, an official historian of the state of Lu and a contemporary of Confucius, were perhaps the best known.

Several historical works were produced in the pre-Qin period, but no attempt was ever made to compile a comprehensive history of the entire past of the nation. The first work of this type was written by Sima Qian (145–87? BC) of the Western Han.

He was the son of an official historian called Sima Tan. On his deathbed the father asked the son to do what he had desired but failed to do—writing a history dealing with all the past events of the whole nation, and the son promised to do that.

Sima Qian was appointed the Grand Historian of the court three years after his father's death. Before this he had travelled far and wide in the country, collecting materials for the book he was to write. In his official position he was able to read the books and documents stored in the court. He began writing his book in 104 BC. Five years later, for some reason he incurred the anger of the emperor

Portrait of Sima Qian

Wu, who made him suffer the punishment of castration. He decided to put up with the shame instead of committing suicide, because he was determined to complete his great work, which he did in 91 BC. Not long after that he died.

Records of the Grand Historian, which he wrote, consists of five parts, 130 chapters, in half a million words. The five parts are: Basic Annals, Chronological Tables, Treatises, Hereditary Houses and Biographies. The first, fourth and fifth parts deal with emperors, big feudal families and famous men respectively. The Chronological Tables are tables of dates of important events; the Treatises are essays devoted to the history and description of various subjects, such as rites, music, and the economy. With minor changes, this arrangement was followed by almost all later official historians in writing dynastic histories.

Records of the Grand Historian

The book was the first general history book published in China, and possibly in the whole world. It covers the major events and personalities of nearly 3,000 years, from the Yellow Emperor down to the writer's day.

The book has great literary value, for it is written in an excellent style. It strengthened the relationship between history and literature.

All kinds of people are described in it: emperors and ministers, sages and philosophers, generals and adventurers, assassins and criminals. Their biographies are very colorful and full of life, with a lot of conversations in direct speech. They have the charm of fiction.

Ban Gu and Sima Qian were often mentioned together by later historians when they discussed the writing of histories. For Ban Gu, the chief author of the *Han Shu* (*Book of Han*), imitated and also introduced innovations in Sima Qian's way of recording historical facts. Sima Qian wrote a general history of several dynasties, while Ban Gu wrote the history of only one dynasty, the Western Han, which was the dynasty preceding his own, the Eastern Han.

Like Sima Qian, Ban Gu (AD 32–92) was born into a

Portrait of Ban Gu

scholar's family. Ban Biao, his father, was a well-known historian who had collected materials with the intention of writing a continuation of Sima Qian's *Records of the Grand Historian*. What he wrote was not extant, but must have been very helpful to his son's work.

Ban Gu's book starts with the first emperor of the Western Han and ends with the emperor who usurped the throne of the last emperor of the dynasty. It covers a history of 229 years. Like Sima Qian's *Records of the Grand Historian*, it contains articles, tables, and biographies, and deals with many aspects of social changes and natural phenomena, with special chapters on morality, the arts, the classics, literature, astronomy, and ghosts and spirits. As it is the history of one dynasty, it is possible for it to give more detailed accounts of events than the *Records of the Grand Historian*.

In his last years, Ban Gu was in a way very close to a powerful man in the court. That man was disloyal to the reigning emperor, and committed suicide after his attempt to kill the emperor failed. Many of his assistants and friends, including Ban Gu, were punished. Ban Gu was thrown into prison. He was then 61, too old to endure the hardships in prison, and died shortly afterwards.

But his book was then only a pile of manuscript. The emperor of the time heard about this, and ordered Ban Gu's sister, Ban Zhao, also an erudite scholar, to edit it. With the help of other

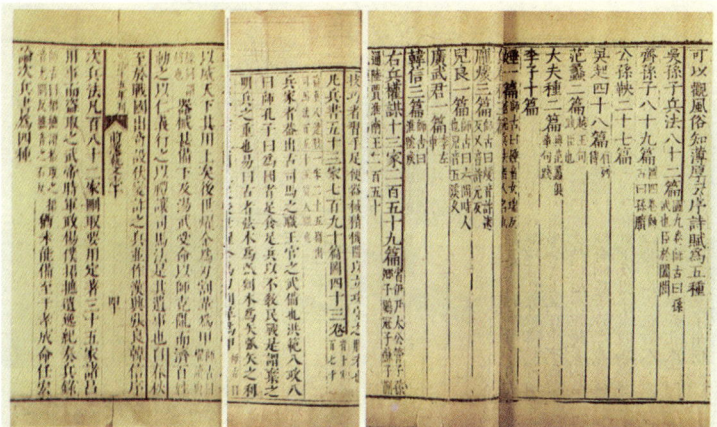

Book of Han

scholars, she completed and finalized her brother's work the *Book of Han*.

It was the first dynastic history, which served as a model to many later historical works. In each dynasty after the Eastern Han, there were official historians who wrote the history of the preceding dynasty. For some dynasties more than one history was written. But only 25 historical works, including Sima Qian's *Records of the Grand Historian* and Ban Gu's *Book of Han*, were generally recognized as official histories. Besides them there were countless historical writings by scholars who were not official historians.

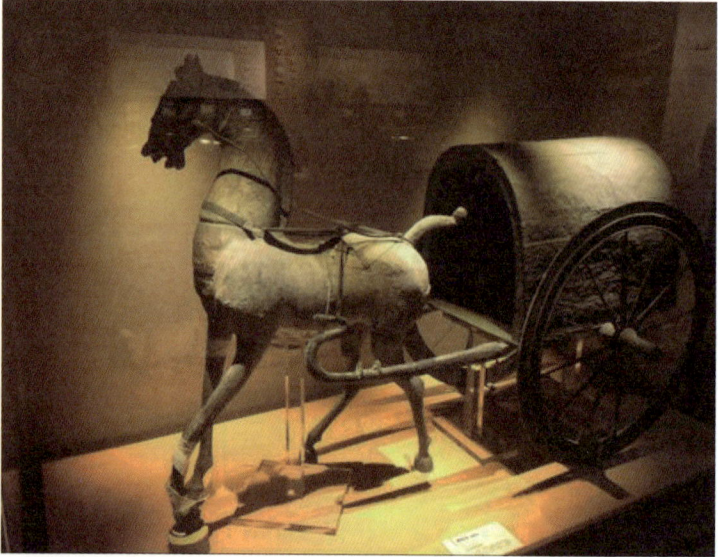

06

Dong Zhongshu and Wang Chong: Two Contradictory Great Philosophers of the Han Dynasties

Qin, one of the seven biggest states in the Warring States Period, grew stronger and stronger by adopting Legalist measures. Finally in 221 BC it conquered all the other states and unified China.

Shihuangdi, or the First Emperor of the Qin, put an end to the 800-year-old system of feudal fiefs. He divided the whole country into a number of prefectures and counties. Their governors and magistrates were appointed by the central government. Land was no longer owned by the nobles; it could be sold and bought.

The emperor did many things to consolidate the unification. He unified weights and measures, the calendar, the currency, and the script. He built highways across the country, dug canals, and built the Great Wall. He did bad things, too, such as burning books and killing scholars by burying them alive.

He and his son, the Second Emperor, oppressed and exploited the common people ruthlessly. They made harsh laws, used severe punishments, collected heavy taxes and forced the people to work for them. They made life so difficult that the people rose in revolt.

The armed revolt led by Chen Sheng and Wu Guang, which began in 209 BC, was the first peasant uprising in Chinese history. It dealt a heavy blow to Qin's rule. Then the armies led by Liu Bang and Xiang Yu overthrew the Qin, which had ruled China only for 15 years. Liu and Xiang fought against each other for four years for the throne. In the end Liu won, and he founded the Han Dynasty (202 BC). This dynasty, also called the Western Han, was to last for about 200 years, and collapsed in revolts and wars. Then Liu Xiu restored the Han Dynasty, moved the capital from Chang'an to Luoyang, and started the Eastern Han.

Under Emperor Wu (156–87 BC), the Western Han reached the peak of its power. The Western Regions were opened. This made it possible for merchants to travel between China and Europe by way of West Asia. China's silk was the main commodity transported along this road, so it was called the

Portrait of Emperor Wu

Silk Road. It played an important part in promoting trade and cultural exchanges between the East and the West.

Having founded a unified, centralized and authoritarian empire, the Han rulers felt the need of a philosophy that could guide and strengthen their rule. They knew that political unification had to be supported by the unification of thought. Not long before them, the First Emperor of the Qin Dynasty had made an attempt to unify thought. He had given orders that books be burnt and scholars be buried alive, and that the people be

Silk Road relic presented in the exhibition "When the Silk Road Meets the Renaissance" held at the National Museum of China

prohibited from the study of anything but the laws then in force. However, he had failed to achieve his goal. Only 15 years after he had unified the country, the dynasty he had founded was toppled, and various schools of thought were active again. This made the Han rulers realize that they ought to unify thought along different lines. Seventy years after the founding of the dynasty, Emperor Wu called on all scholars to present suggestions about effective government. He got valuable opinions from an outstanding scholar of the time.

Portrait of Dong Zhongshu

His name was Dong Zhongshu (179–104 BC). He presented three memorials to the emperor, recommending a series of theories and policies. The emperor was impressed and used him as a high-ranking official. But later he offended the emperor and was imprisoned for some time. After he was released, he devoted his time to writing and teaching. It was said that he worked so hard that for three years he did not take a look at his own garden.

He suggested that Confucianism be made the orthodox philosophy, or official belief, and that all other schools of thought be discredited. Emperor Wu accepted this suggestion. This decision had a tremendous influence on the development of Chinese culture, for it put Confucianism into a dominant position. From then on, in most dynasties, most scholars studied Confucianism, and only confucian scholars were qualified to be officials in the government. But the Han rulers did not ban the teaching and discussion of other schools of thought. This policy was also followed by later dynasties.

Dong Zhongshu was also known for the "three cardinal guides and five constant virtues" he advocated. The three cardinal guides were: the prince was the guide of his ministers, the father was the guide of his sons, and the husband was the guide of his wife. The five constant virtues were: humanity, rightness, propriety, wisdom and trustworthiness. These principles were to become an important part of the feudal ethical code and the theoretical basis of feudal rule.

According to Dong Zhongshu, Heaven had its will and purpose. It was Heaven that made the sun, the moon, and the stars move, the four seasons change, and all animals and plants grow and die. Heaven was kindhearted, so it made things produce one another; Heaven was also severe, so it made things overcome one another. Moreover, Heaven created a ruler to rule over the people. This meant that Heaven wanted the people to be ruled. When a ruler did something wrong, Heaven would be angry and would give the ruler warnings by causing strange natural phenomena to happen, such as eclipses, earthquakes, floods and droughts.

This theory—the interaction between Heaven and man—had a clear purpose. On the one hand, it was intended to show that a ruler's position and power were given by Heaven, and should not be questioned; on the other hand, the ruler should be virtuous and benevolent, and govern well, so as not to incur Heaven's anger. Dong had a well-known saying, "The Way is great because it originates in Heaven. Heaven does not change; nor does the Way."

Dong Zhongshu was no doubt the most important philosopher of the Western Han. During the Eastern Han that followed it, his theories, especially that of the interaction between Heaven and man, were criticized and refuted by a brave scholar—

Wang Chong (about 27–97). Wang's grandfather was a merchant and his father a peasant. Born in Shangyu near the better-known city of Shaoxing, he studied at a private school, where he was taught some Confucian classics in his childhood. As a young man he went to Luoyang, the capital, and stayed there for some time. He was too poor to buy books, and had to go to bookstores to browse what books he could find. Somehow he became a pupil of Ban Biao, a famous scholar and the father of Ban Gu, who edited the *Book of Han*. Later, Wang was given the post of a petty official in a local government. By far more learned than his superiors, he found it hard to obey their orders. So he resigned and returned to his hometown to teach students and write books for the rest of his life.

Only one of the books he wrote is now extant. It is called *Balanced Discussions*, on which he spent over 30 years. The book shows his remarkable scientific skepticism, and his courage in fighting the powerful influence of the ideas of Dong Zhongshu and his followers.

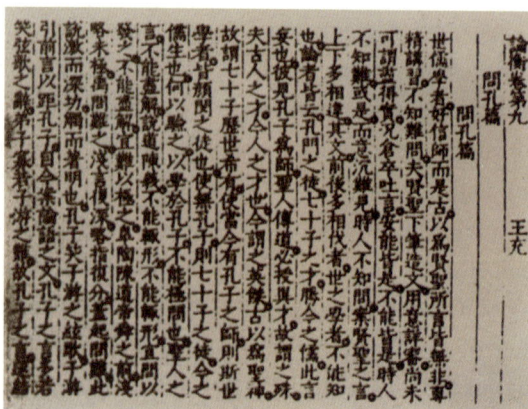

Balanced Discussions

Wang Chong regarded Heaven and earth as part of nature. They were made of *qi*, or material force. It was material force that gave birth to all the things in the universe, and this process was spontaneous and natural. No one or nothing controlled or directed the birth, growth and change of things in the

Statue of Meng Jiangnv

universe. Heaven took no conscious or purposeful action. Man could not affect Heaven in any way, nor could Heaven react to man's behavior or action. Unusual natural phenomena like earthquakes occurred spontaneously; they had nothing to do with the policies or mistakes of rulers. There were coincidences, which made some people think they were related. For instance, legend had it that Meng Jiangnv cried so sadly that as a result the Great Wall collapsed. In fact, it was when the Great Wall was collapsing that Meng Jiangnv happened to be crying near it. The two events were not connected at all.

According to Dong Zhongshu, Heaven was most humane, so it gave warnings to rulers when they made mistakes. Wang Chong said that this view was illogical. If Heaven was humane, it would in the first place give the people only good rulers. It would not consider it necessary to put a bad ruler on the throne and let him do wrong things, and then give him warnings.

Wang Chong stressed the importance of effect in testing the correctness of a theory. He said, "However elaborate and high-sounding a theory may be, it should not be believed if it is different from what things really are and cannot produce the effect it is supposed to produce." In other words, an action should be tested by its effect, and a theory should be proved by fact.

He also had his own ideas about human nature. He said most people had to be educated to be good. He was against the view that people of high position and wealth were all good and poor people were all evil. Whether one was rich or poor was not determined by his moral standard. The rich were rich only because they robbed the poor, and officials used their power for selfish purposes. Confucius, he said, did not get the treatment he deserved in his lifetime, and Yan Hui, a perfectly virtuous man, died young because he was poor.

He discussed many other questions in *Balanced Discussions*, and many of his views were original and critical. But his views, though sound and profound, did not exert a great influence on scholars, let alone common people of later ages. The reason was obvious. The feudal rulers of all later dynasties naturally liked Dong Zhongshu's ideas, which were helpful to them, and hated Wang Chong's, which would make people think independently. Emperor Qianlong of the Qing Dynasty, for instance, called Wang Chong a man who wanted to "denounce the sages and destroy the Way."

07

*The Coming of Buddhism
to China*

In ancient India there were many small states with different languages and traditions. South of the Himalayas, in the southern part of present-day Nepal, there was a state ruled by the Sakya clan. One year in the 6th century BC, the king of the state, who had been longing for a child for many years, happily got a son. The king named the boy Siddhartha, which meant "every wish fulfilled."

Near the king's castle there lived a prophet. He came and begged to see the child. On seeing him, he predicted that the prince might give up the court life and become a buddha (the awakened one) to save the world.

One day when he was seven, the prince went out of the palace with his father. They were watching a farmer plowing a field when he noticed a bird come down to the ground and carry off a small worm turned up by the farmer's plow. He asked himself, "Do all living creatures kill one another like this?"

He grew up to be a quiet young man, often lost in thought, taking no interest in the luxurious life of the palace. The king was worried, and tried in every possible way to cheer up his son. When he was 19, the king arranged his marriage. The king also gave orders that the prince be entertained with all kinds of nice things and that he should be prevented from seeing any suffering of the people outside the palace.

But still he saw some suffering that accompanied life, such as an old man who could not walk properly, a sick man about to die, and a dead man being carried to his grave. These sights made him think all the more deeply, and urged him to try to understand the true meaning of life.

When he was 29, his only son was born. Then one night he left the palace to become a homeless mendicant, determined to

Sakyamuni giving a sermon

find a solution to his spiritual unrest. This was called the "great renunciation."

He wandered from place to place and talked with many hermits and wise, learned men. While practising asceticism rigorously, he had long meditations. Six years passed. Finally, he came to a forest and continued to meditate there, though he was very weak and was in danger of losing his life. One morning, the struggle was over. His mind was clear and bright like the day. He had at last found the path to Enlightenment. He became the Buddha at the age of 35.

From then on he went all over the states to teach men the truth he had found. More and more people accepted it and became his disciples or followers. He was respectfully called Sakyamuni (the sage of the Sakyas).

He preached for 45 years until he was 80 years old. He was very ill and knew he would be passing into nirvana, but he continued teaching his disciples in his last moments. After he died, his body was cremated. Several states wanted to have his relics, so they were divided into eight parts, each of which was

Baoxiang Temple, where a tooth of the Buddha is kept

given to a state. One of his teeth was later brought to China and has been kept in a pagoda in a temple near Beijing.

According to Buddhism, everything in the world is brought about by causes and effects, and everything disappears when its causes and effects disappear or change. Rain falls, plants grow, flowers blossom—all these natural phenomena are the results of certain causes, and they change when the causes change.

The life of a person is also the result of causes and conditions. His parents give birth to him; he is nourished by food; his mind is developed by education and experience. So one's flesh and spirit are related to conditions, and they change as conditions change.

A cause produces an effect, and the effect is the cause of another effect. In other words, all the things and phenomena in the world are connected with, dependent on and conditioned by one another. So it is said in one Buddhist scripture, "There is this, so there is that; this arises, so that arises; when this is not, that is not; this ceases, so that ceases." Causes and effects go on forever—there is no beginning and there is no end. This is where Buddhism is different from some other religions. It does not hold that the universe was created by a god.

As the world is made up of causes and effects, it follows that nothing in the world is permanent. Everything is transient. Just as pictures are drawn by artists, real, stable things and their surroundings are created by the mind. The mind considers this good and that bad, but in fact there is no such distinction. For instance, the process of life and the process of death are the same. What is called the east is also the west.

Similarly, a person is not something permanent or stable either. A person is only a combination of ever-changing physical and mental elements or forces. Every moment something is born, grows, decays or dies in him. What a person is today is not what he or she was yesterday. It is only ignorance that makes people believe that there is a permanent "self" or "individual."

In connection with human life, Sakyamuni preached the "Four Noble Truths":

1. The truth of suffering. Life is suffering. Birth, old age, sickness and death are all sufferings. To meet a person whom one hates, to be separated from a person whom one loves, to seek something that cannot be obtained, and physical and mental pains are all sufferings.

Sakyamuni came to the conclusion that life is suffering perhaps because in his time the common people and the slaves in India had a bad lot and really suffered a great deal, and he had deep sympathy for them.

2. The truth of the cause of suffering. The cause of suffering is desire, or thirst, or greed. The body and the mind desire pleasures; they desire existence and becoming. Because man is ignorant, he does not know that life and man himself are both impermanent. Therefore he is filled with worldly passions and always tries to seek what he feels desirable. This gives rise to all sufferings.

3. The truth of the cessation of suffering. If desire can be removed, all human suffering will come to an end. The ideal state where there is no desire, no passion and no suffering is called nirvana, which means freedom from the endless cycle of personal reincarnations.

4. The truth of the right path. To attain nirvana, one has to follow the right path. It consists of the following: right view, right thought, right speech, right behavior, right livelihood, right effort, right mindfulness, and right concentration.

a Buddhist wall painting in Dunhuang Grottoes

Reincarnation is an important tenet of Buddhism. Whatever one thinks, says or does is his karma. The effect of one's karma cannot be removed. It leads to corresponding reward or retribution in his present life and will decide his fate in his next existence. It is possible for a man to be reborn as a man, and it is also possible for him to be reborn as a ghost or an animal. Such reincarnation goes on until a person attains nirvana.

Buddhism was first introduced into China at the beginning of the Eastern Han, or about 2,000 years ago. This had something to do with the opening of the Western Regions, which made travel between China and India easier than before. In 67, two Indian monks came to Luoyang, the capital. Emperor Ming ordered the

White Horse Temple, Henan Province

building of a temple, which was named White Horse Temple, and asked the Indian monks to translate Buddhist scriptures into Chinese there. They were followed by other monks from India and West Asia. At first, Buddhism was known only to members of the upper classes. It was during the period of the Southern and Northern Dynasties that it was spread among the ordinary people.

08

Pure Talk and
Mysterious Learning

Towards the end of the Eastern Han Dynasty, the rulers were either weak or corrupt. There was continuous power struggle in the court, and the common people were badly oppressed and exploited. What had happened at the end of the Qin and the Western Han happened again: peasants rose in revolt in many parts of the country. One peasant army led by Zhang Jiao was active in North China. As a mark each fighter of the army wound a yellow turban around his head, and this gave the army a name: the Yellow Turbans.

The Han rulers had to rely on local armies in fighting against the peasants. After many years of war, the Yellow Turbans were suppressed, and three of the local army leaders divided the country among them: Cao Cao in the north, Sun Quan in the southeast, and Liu Bei in the southwest. The kingdoms they founded were called Wei, Wu and Shu respectively. These three kingdoms lasted about 60 years before China was again unified by the Jin. Sima Yan, the most powerful minister of the Wei government, had usurped the throne and changed the name of the dynasty to Jin.

Battle of Red Cliffs—Painting at the Long Corridor of the Summer Palace

Sima Yan's son could not rule the country effectively. Internal strife arose and border tribes from the north and northwest invaded North China. One of them occupied Luoyang, the capital, and put an end to the Jin or Western Jin. Some members of the Sima house and many nobles fled south and founded the Eastern Jin in the Changjiang River valley. In the north, northwest, and Sichuan altogether 16 small states ruled different areas at different times.

The Eastern Jin was replaced by the Song, which was taken over by the Qi, Qi by Liang and Liang by Chen. These four dynasties, called the Southern Dynasties, were in existence for about 170 years (420–589).

In the north, various small states were conquered by the Northern Wei in 386. It was divided into the Eastern Wei and Western Wei. They were replaced by the Northern Qi and Northern Zhou. These five dynasties were collectively called the Northern Dynasties.

In 581 Yang Jian, prime minister of the Northern Zhou, seized power and established the Sui Dynasty. In 589 he conquered the Chen in the south and unified China.

Before that North China had been under the rule of various border tribes for nearly three centuries. This led to a large-scale merging of cultures. On the whole, those tribes adopted the culture of the Han people. One Xianbei ruler, for instance, ordered his people to stop using the Xianbei language and wearing the traditional Xianbei clothing, and to use the Han language and clothing instead. Moreover, he wanted his people to adopt Han surnames. At the same time, the Han people also absorbed some aspects of the culture of the tribes.

A porcelain bowl with pure talk decoration

During the Wei and Jin period, Confucianism no longer enjoyed a predominant position as it had during the two Han dynasties. The rulers then had no urgent need for scholars who stressed the importance of moral principles and humane government, because it was an unstable and turbulent age. Instead, they needed capable strategists and men who could help them to seize and consolidate power. On the other hand, many scholars were disgusted with the Cao and Sima families pretending to be upright and virtuous while fighting against each other for power and persecuting those who were critical of them. These scholars dared not oppose the rulers; they wanted to keep themselves away from political strife. Some of them adopted an uncommon and even strange way of life, and often talked in an unusual manner. Here are two examples of their strange behavior and conversation:

Ji Kang enjoyed doing the work of a blacksmith. One day he was forging something out of a piece of iron under a big tree in front of his house, when Zhong Hui, a well-known scholar-official, came to visit him. Ji Kang saw him, but he did not stop his work to greet him. A moment later Zhong turned to go. Then Ji asked him, "What did you hear that made you come? And what have you seen here that makes you leave?" Zhong answered, "Before I came, I heard what I heard. When I leave, I've seen

Portrait of Ji Kang

what I've seen."

Wang Huizhi lived in Shanyin. One night it was snowing heavily. Suddenly he thought of his friend Dai Kui. He hired a boat and it took him the whole night to get to Dai's place. As soon as he reached Dai's house, he turned and ordered the boatman to take him back. When asked the reason, he replied, "I started the trip on the spur of the moment, and I returned when the spur was over. There was no need to see Dai."

These scholars were more interested in the *Lao Zi*, the *Zhuang Zi* and the *Book of Changes* than any other classics. They called these three books "Three Mysterious Classics." From the ideas in these works they developed what was called "mysterious learning." The term comes from one line in the *Lao Zi*, "Mystery of all mysteries! The door of all subtleties!" They discussed such concepts as being and nonbeing, and the ethical code and spontaneity, the meaning of language and the real intention of the author.

Cao Cao, who founded the Kingdom of Wei, and his two sons Cao Pi and Cao Zhi, were also famous poets. For a time they were leaders of the literary scene.

Liu Xie wrote *Literary Mind and the Carving of the Dragon*, which set forth a series of principles of literary criticism. This and many other similar books showed the writers of that time realized the necessity of looking into their own works and literature in general.

Of all the literary men of the time perhaps Tao Yuanming (365?–427) had a most lasting influence. Having served in the government for a short time, he left his post because he was not willing to "bow to a child" (referring to a superior). Henceforward he lived and worked as a farmer.

Appreciating Chrysanthemums by the Eastern Hedge,
by Tang Yin of the Ming Dynasty

"I stayed in the cage for a long time, and now I have returned to nature." he wrote. The "cage" meant his official life. Nature was his salvation.

In many of his poems he described his farmer's life, such as:

I sowed beans below the south mountain,
The weeds were so heavy and the beans so sparse.
I got up at dawn to weed out,
And returned with the moon and the hoe.
The roads are narrow and the evening dew wetted my
clothes.
What did I care about my clothes
So long as I held on to my wishes?

种豆南山下，草盛豆苗稀。
晨兴理荒秽，带月荷锄归。
道狭草木长，夕露沾我衣。
衣沾不足惜，但使愿无违。

In poems like this Tao Yuanming expressed his preference of down to earth's labour to an official's life.

The Taoist religion took shape towards the end of the Eastern Han. There were the Five-*Dou*-of-Rice sect and the Taiping sect. The former was started by Zhang Ling in Sichuan and the latter by Zhang Jiao who led the Yellow Turban uprisings. Both sects were suppressed during the period of the Three Kingdoms, but the religion did not die. During the Jin Dynasty and the period of the Southern and Northern Dynasties, the religion spread in the upper classes and among the common people. Some leaders and scholars of the religion wrote theoretical books, and created rituals, regulations and organizational systems for the religion. They gave the religion a definite form and a theoretical basis.

The Taoist religion originated with the ancient secret ways of becoming immortals and drawing magic figures for driving away evil spirits and bringing happiness. *Dao*, according to the religion, is the origin of the universe and the basis of everything. Lao Zi's *Dao De Jing* is a sacred book to its members, who worship a great number of gods and immortals, Lao Zi being one of the most important among them. It also has special ways of self-cultivation and self-preservation.

It was said that there were three religions in China: Confucianism, Buddhism and Taoism. This statement, however, is not accurate. Confucianism is a belief, not a religion, as it does not have a god or a religious organization. Taoism refers to two things: the philosophy founded by Lao Zi, Zhuang Zi and other thinkers, and the Taoist religion, which is in a way connected with but essentially different from the philosophy. It would be more scientific to say that in the past there were in China two main schools of philosophy—Confucianism and Taoism—and two religions—Buddhism and the Taoist religion.

09

Chan (Zen) Buddhism

Buddhism was widely spread during the period of the Southern and Northern Dynasties. Both in the South and in the North, a great number of temples were built, and many Buddhist sutras were translated into Chinese. Moreover, new Buddhist theories and a few Chinese sects of Buddhism were founded.

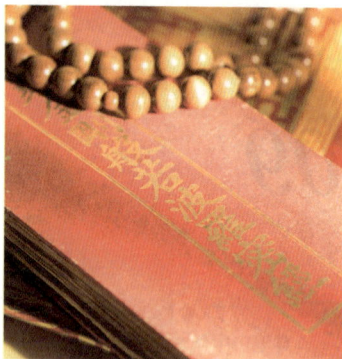
Buddhist scriptures

This trend continued during the Sui and Tang dynasties, when more new Buddhist sects emerged. They inherited and elaborated original Indian Buddhism and at the same time developed Buddhist theories that were essentially Chinese.

One common character of these Chinese sects was that they tried to incorporate into their tenets part of Taoist philosophy and part of Confucianism, in an effort to merge the three philosophies. Their doctrines, especially those of Huayan and Zen, may be called Chinese Buddhism, because they were quite different from Indian Buddhism. What follows is a brief story of the beginning of Zen Buddhism.

Its history began with the coming of Bodhidharma to China from Southern India in 520. He was a learned monk and was determined to spread Buddhism in China. He came by sea and when he arrived in Guangzhou, the emperor of the Liang (the third of the four southern dynasties), who believed in Buddhism, invited him to Nanjing, the capital. But they disagreed in their first meeting, so the Indian monk left Nanjing and went further north to the state of Wei. He preached in the area between Luoyang and Mount Songshan, where well-known Shaolin Temple was located.

Shaolin Temple, Henan Province

Bodhidharma's main teaching was to attain Buddhahood by way of meditation. Those who aspired to enlightenment should isolate themselves from the outside world and concentrate on their own thinking. He held that all people originally had Buddha nature, which they could discover in themselves if they got rid of all impure thoughts. The Sanskrit word for meditation was *dhyana*, which was translated into Chinese as *chan*. So this sect of Buddhism came to be called Chan Buddhism. The name Zen Buddhism, a Japanese term, has been more commonly used abroad.

Bodhidharma was regarded as the first patriarch of this sect. Its fifth patriarch was a monk called Hongren. He preached in a temple in Huangmei, in eastern Hubei. His two prominent disciples, Shenxiu and Huineng, especially the latter, enriched the theory of the sect and made it known throughout the country.

Huineng (638–713) was born in Guangdong. His father died when he was young, and he supported his mother by collecting and selling firewood. One day he heard a man reciting a Buddhist sutra on the street and was deeply touched by the words. He asked the man where he had learned it. The man told him the name of a temple in Huangmei, Hubei. Immediately he decided to go there. After making arrangements for his mother's daily life, he started.

It took him a month to get to the temple. When he went to see Hongren, the master asked him, "Where do you come from, and what do you want to do here?"

"I'm from the South, and want to become a Buddha." he answered.

"The Southerners have no Buddha nature. How could you expect to attain Buddhahood?"

"There may be Southerners and Northerners, but as far as Buddha nature goes, there is no distinction between them."

This answer pleased the master, who allowed him to stay, and told him to work as a rice pounder in the temple.

Some time later, the master thought it was time for him to choose a successor, for he was very old. He announced that the disciple who wrote a gatha (short poem) expressing a thorough understanding of Buddhist principles would be named the next patriarch. Most of the monks in the temple believed that Shenxiu would write one and be chosen. After a few days of hard thinking, Shenxiu wrote the following poem on a wall:

The body is a bodhi tree,
The mind is a bright mirror.
They need dusting from time to time,
So that no dirt may gather.

身是菩提树，
心如明镜台。
时时勤拂拭，
莫使染尘埃。

When the master saw the poem, he commented, "He has not seen the truth yet. More meditation is necessary."

Huineng, who was illiterate, heard his fellow monks talking about the poem, and composed one to comment on it. He asked someone to write his poem on the wall:

Originally the bodhi is not a tree,
Neither is there a bright mirror.
Since originally there is nothing,
Where can dirt gather?

菩提本无树，
明镜亦非台。
本来无一物，
何处染尘埃？

When the master saw this poem, he knew that Huineng had a deeper understanding of the truth. He appointed him the sixth patriarch. As there were many jealous monks in the temple, the master told Huineng to go back to Guangdong and live in hiding, to wait for an opportunity to reveal his status and perform his duties.

Back in Guangdong, Huineng lived a secluded life in the mountains for many years. Then one day, when he was 39 years old, he went to a temple to listen to the learned abbot's explanation of Buddhism. Two monks were arguing on the fluttering of a pennant. One said "The pennant is fluttering." and the other said "The wind is fluttering the pennant." Huineng interrupted them by saying, "Neither the pennant nor the wind is moving. It is your own

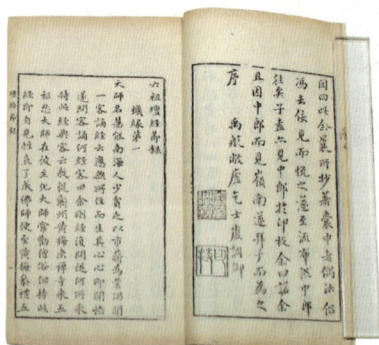

Scripture from the Platform

mind that is moving." The abbot heard this remark and was surprised, so he invited the stranger in and began to talk with him.

In this way Huineng's status as the sixth patriarch of the Zen sect was known. Shortly afterwards he started preaching in a temple in Shaoguan in northern Guangdong. His talks on Buddhism were recorded by some of his disciples. These talks made up a book entitled *Scripture from the Platform*, which contained the basic theories of the Zen sect.

As has been mentioned, Zen followers believed that everyone possessed Buddha nature, but owing to the confusion of thought, they failed to realize this. To seek enlightenment, one should not rely on the study of scriptures, but on the discovery of one's own Buddha nature.

It was possible for one to awaken to the truth in an instant, and the moment he was enlightened, all his confused thoughts would vanish, and he would become a Buddha. This theory of instant awakening was directly opposed to Shenxiu's theory of gradual awakening, which was reflected in the short poem he wrote in the temple in Huangmei.

Zen principles were summarized in these four lines, "The belief is passed on outside the religion. There is no reliance on written scripts. It goes straight into people's minds. One becomes a Buddha the moment he sees his own Buddha nature."

For some time, Shenxiu and Huineng led respectively the northern and southern schools of the Zen sect, or the school of gradual awakening and that of instant awakening. But the southern school was more influential than the northern one.

Later Zen Buddhism was spread to Japan, Korea and some western countries.

10

Tang Poetry
and Major Tang Poets

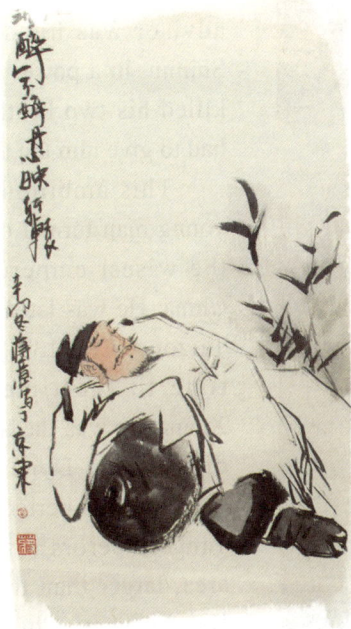

In 581 Yang Jian, prime minister of the Northern Zhou, seized power and established the Sui Dynasty. Eight years later he unified China after he conquered Chen in the south, thus putting an end to the period of division which lasted more than three centuries.

His son, who succeeded him, was a corrupt and evil emperor. His despotic rule was hated by the people, and peasant uprisings started. The dynasty was overthrown only 37 years after it was founded.

Portrait of Li Yuan

Portrait of Li Shimin

Li Yuan, a military commander in Taiyuan, Shanxi, raised an army and occupied Chang'an. In 618 he founded the Tang Dynasty. His chief advisor was his second son, Li Shimin. In a power struggle Shimin killed his two brothers; his father had to give him the throne.

This ambitious and capable young man turned out to be one of the wisest emperors of ancient China. He was later called Emperor Taizong. The 130 years from his time to the time of Emperor Xuanzong was the heyday not only of the Tang Dynasty, but of the whole feudal period of China. The Tang emperors ruled over a vast area, larger than that ruled by the Han Dynasty. China was then the largest and strongest country in the world; it was also economically and culturally the most advanced. In Chang'an, the capital, there were over 300,000 households, with a great number of merchants, traders, scholars and students from foreign countries. Chinese culture, including philosophy, and political, legal and economic systems, had a far-reaching influence, especially in East Asia. At the same time, foreign products and culture were introduced into China.

In 755 the revolt of An Lushan and Shi Siming broke out. Their troops entered Chang'an, and Emperor Xuanzong fled to Sichuan in a hurry. This was the beginning of the decline of the Tang Dynasty. But the dynasty, though shaky, continued to rule China for another 150 years, and came to an end in 907.

Chinese poetry has a very long history. The *Book of Songs*, the first collection of folk songs and poems, was compiled before Confucius' time, for he mentioned the book and asked his students to study it several times. Most of the poems in the book were composed during the Western Zhou period, or the 1,000 years before Confucius. It was said that the Zhou rulers sent officials to different parts of the country to collect folk songs. They were then presented to the rulers, who tried to judge the sentiments and views of the people by them.

The *Book of Songs* marked the beginning of Chinese literature, and also the beginning of realism in literature. Many of the 305 poems in the book deal with

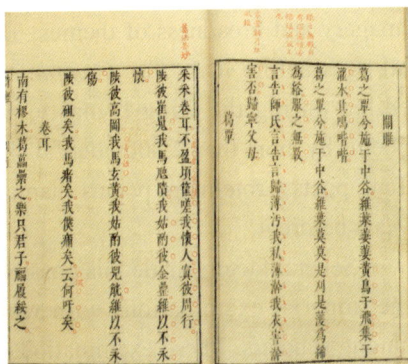

Book of Songs

the lives of the common people, their daily occupations, their joys and sorrows, their hard work and duties in wars.

Then in the Warring States period the state of Chu in the south produced a great poet—Qu Yuan (340–278 BC). He was the first Chinese poet whose name we know. When he saw that his state was approaching ruin and yet he could do nothing to save it, he drowned himself in the Miluo River near Lake Dongting. His representative work is the *Li Sao* (*Sorrows at Departure*), which is a long poem describing his love for his state and his disappointment at its situation. The poem marks the beginning of romanticism in Chinese poetry, as it contains descriptions of imagined scenes in Heaven.

During the period of the two Han dynasties and the period of the Southern and Northern Dynasties, many poets wrote poems with five-character lines. Outstanding among them were Cao Cao and his two sons, and Tao Qian. There were beautiful poems whose writers were unknown, such as the *Nineteen Ancient Poems* and "Southeastward Flies the Peacock."

The Tang Dynasty was the golden age of Chinese poetry. In the number of poems and variety of forms, in the beauty of imagery and broadness of themes, Tang poetry surpassed that of all ages before it. In *The Complete Anthology of Tang Poetry*, edited during the Qing Dynasty, are collected nearly 50,000 poems by more than 2,000 poets. This means that in 300 years the Tang poets wrote more poems than all the poets had in the 2,000 years before it.

Several factors made this possible. The Sui rulers had started the imperial examinations with which to select officials from among scholars. These examinations were continued in the Tang Dynasty. As a result, many people, mainly landlords' children,

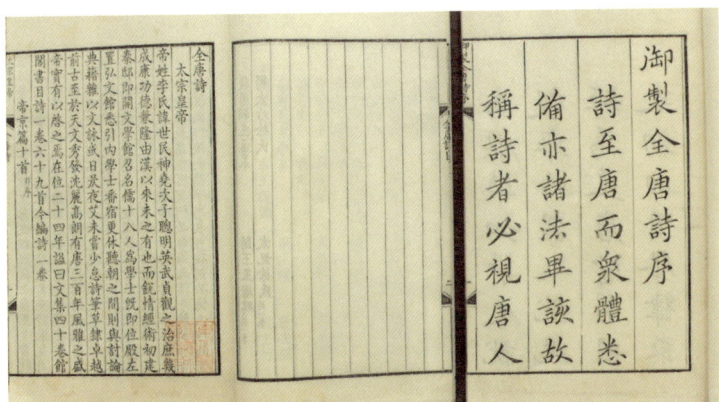

The Complete Anthology of Tang Poetry

studied hard to sit for the examinations, which required writing poems. Besides, there was to a certain extent freedom of thought; Confucianism, Taoism and Buddhism were all studied and discussed by scholars. The unification of the country made it possible for scholars to travel north and south, increasing their contacts and experience and broadening their vision. Foreign arts, especially those of West and Central Asia, were introduced into Central China, and they enriched the cultural life of the Han people. Finally, from the Western Zhou to the Southern and Northern Dynasties, Chinese poetry had been developing and had become rich in content and form. This long history provided conditions for the blossoming of Tang poetry.

This long tradition had two clear features: one was that folk songs or *yuefu* were the main origin of the different poetic forms; the other was that realism was the main tendency. Most poets were concerned about the conditions of the country and the life of the people.

Among the most famous Tang poets are Li Bai, Du Fu and

Portrait of Li Bai

Bai Juyi.

Li Bai (701–762) was born in Suiye in Central Asia, which belonged to Tang Empire. His ancestors had been banished there by the Sui rulers. At five he moved to Sichuan with his father, who was probably a rich merchant. When young, he studied not only Confucian classics, but works of other schools. After 20 he first travelled far and wide in Sichuan, and then he started a long journey to Central, East and North China. He did not sit for the imperial examinations, for he looked down upon it. But he wished to become an official. When he was 42, he was recommended to Emperor Xuanzong, who ordered him to go to Chang'an. He stayed there for three years and was bitterly disappointed. During the years of An Lushan's rebellion, he joined the staff of Prince Li Lin. Later, because Li Lin tried to seize power but failed, Li Bai was exiled to Yelang, in present day Guizhou Province. On his way to Yelang he was freed by an amnesty. He went to East China and died at 62 in Dangtu, Anhui.

He wrote as many as 900 poems. Some of them describe the life of the people; some describe the magnificent scenery he saw; others express his own wishes and sorrows. His poems are characterized by unusual imagination and free and direct expression of feelings. That is why he is called a romantic poet.

At dawn I left Baidi towering in the midst of colorful clouds,
And reached Jiangling a thousand li away in a day.
The screams of monkeys on either bank went on and on,
While my light boat passed by ten thousand hills.

朝辞白帝彩云间，
千里江陵一日还。
两岸猿声啼不住，
轻舟已过万重山。

Satisfaction and admiration will fill our hearts when we read such beautiful and dashing lines. They are so colorful, musical, and impressive. The image in the poem—a boat rushing forward down the gorges—is just a description of the poet himself.

Three Gorges

Du Fu (712–770) was born in Gong County, Henan. The son of an official, he was interested in learning when he was young. "I've read over ten thousand volumes." he said. At 20 he started his 10-year-long travels from north to south. At 35 he went to Chang'an, where he stayed for ten years without getting any position in the government. His disappointment made him look at reality and see the sharp contrast between the life of the upper classes and that of the ordinary people. He began to write poems about the sufferings of the poor. After An Lushan's rebellion began, he had a hard time as a refugee, but this brought him closer to the people. His well-known poems describing three officials and three departures were written during this period. In 759 he went to Chengdu. After wandering in Sichuan, Hubei and Hunan for more than ten years, he finally died on board a small boat on his way from Changsha to Yueyang.

Deep sympathy for the people is one of the main

Portrait of Du Fu

characteristics of Du Fu's poems. In this respect he surpassed all earlier poets. His poems have been called "poetic history", for they reflect the political and military situation of his time, and the life and miseries of the people. He pushed the tradition of realism in poetry to a new level.

Here are the first six lines from the poem "The Official of Shihao":

At dusk I came to Shihao Village to stay overnight,
And heard an official trying to catch someone after dark.
The old man in the house climbed over the wall and fled,
Leaving the old woman to face the official at the door.
Shouting loudly, the official was very angry;
Sobbing bitterly, the woman was full of sorrow.

暮投石壕村，有吏夜捉人。
老翁逾墙走，老妇出门看。
吏呼一何怒，妇啼一何苦。

Du Fu exposes the shameless luxury of the ruling class in these famous lines:

Behind the red doors wine and meat stink,
But on the roads lie men frozen to death.

朱门酒肉臭，路有冻死骨。

Li Bai and Du Fu are among the greatest poets that China has produced. Their poems have given the Chinese people boundless inspiration and have been taken as models of poetry. Han Yu, also a famous Tang poet, wrote: "The works of Li and Du are there; their brilliant light will shine forever."

Two years after Du Fu died, another great poet was born. Bai Juyi (772–846), the son of a petty official, was born in Xinzheng, Henan. He spent his youth wandering about to escape wars, and was often cold and hungry. He was successful in imperial examinations, became an official, and worked in the central government for about 15 years. Then because he was disliked by those in power, he was sent to work in Jiangzhou (now Jiujiang), Hangzhou and Suzhou. Later he moved to Luoyang, where he died at the age of 75.

Bai Juyi wrote more poems than any other Tang poet—nearly 3,000. Many of them deal with important social and political problems, and show signs of Du Fu's influence. He also wrote many lyrics expressing his personal feelings. His two long narrative poems—"The Everlasting Sorrow" and "The Song of a *Pipa* Player"—are among the best known.

Portrait of Bai Juyi

Many of his poems have deep meaning, and they are written in simple and plain language, which ordinary readers can understand.

The following are a few lines from "The Old Man with a Broken Arm":

In the south and in the north of my village people wept sadly;
Children were parting from parents and husbands from wives.
Everyone said that in battles against the southern tribes,
Of ten thousand men sent there not one returned.

村南村北哭声哀，儿别爷娘夫别妻。
皆云前后征蛮者，千万人行无一回。

The poem clearly shows the poet's opposition to battles against border tribes, which caused miseries to both Han and tribal people.

In "The Song of a *Pipa* Player," there are these lines describing the beautiful music produced by the *Pipa* player:

Strong and loud, the thick string sounded like a sudden shower;
Weak and soft, the thin string whispered in your ear.
When strong and weak, loud and soft sounds were mixed,
They were like big and tiny pearls falling on a jade plate.

大弦嘈嘈如急雨，小弦切切如私语。
嘈嘈切切错杂弹，大珠小珠落玉盘。

Tang poetry is indeed an inexhaustible treasury. In every sense it is the peak of Chinese poetry. The Chinese people are rightly proud of this incomparable heritage.

Song of Pipa *at* Xunyang, by Qiu Ying of the Ming Dynasty

11

Tang Prose and Fiction: The Literary Reform Movement of the Tang Dynasty and the Development of Fiction

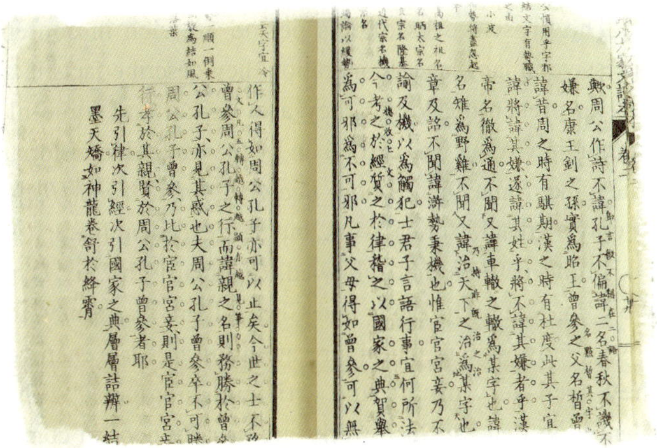
歟周公作詩不諱孔子不偏諱二名春秋不譏不
嫌名康王釗之孫實爲昭王曾參之父名晳曾
諱昔周之時有騏期漢之時有杜度此其子宜
諱將諱其嫌遂諱其姓乎將不諱其嫌者乎漢
帝名徹爲通不聞又諱車轍之轍爲某字也諱
名雉爲野雞不聞又諱治天下之治爲某字也
章及詔不聞諱滸勢秉機也惟宦官宮妾乃不
諭及機以爲觸犯士君子言語行事宜何所法
今考之於經質之於律稽之以國家之典賀舉
爲可邪爲不可邪凡事父母得如曾參可以無
作人得如周公孔子亦可以止矣今世之士不
曾參周公孔子之行而諱親之名則務勝於曾
公孔子亦見其惑也夫周公孔子曾參卒不可勝
周公孔子曾參乃比於宦官宮妾則是宦官宮
行孝於其親賢於周公孔子曾參者耶
先引律次引經次引國家之典層層詰辯一結
墨天矯如神龍卷舒於絳霄

Prose started very early in China. In the *Book of History* there are articles that may have been written during the Shang Dynasty, or more than three thousand years ago. During the Spring and Autumn and Warring States period, there was a rapid development of prose. Many writers appeared and important prose works were written. These works fall into two main types: historical and philosophical. Among the former are the *Zuo Zhuan* (Commentary on the *Spring and Autumn Annals* by Zuo Qiuming), *Conversations from the States*, and *Stratagems of the Warring States*. Among the latter are *The Analects*, *The Book of Mencius*, the *Zhuang Zi*, the *Xun Zi*, the *Han Fei Zi*, and so on. (The *Lao Zi* is written in verse.)

The blossoming of prose during this period was mainly due to two factors: the great social changes happening at the time and the emancipation of people's thought. Both the social order and the political structure were then in a process of change and, as a result, people, especially scholars, had all kinds of new ideas and beliefs. These provided rich material for the historians and the philosophers, who usually wanted to express their views.

The prose works of this period are rich in content and expressive in language. In narration they describe facts in a vivid way; in presenting views they are logical and forceful. This tradition in writing was carried on by the early Han historians and writers like Sima Qian, whose *Records of the Grand Historian* is not only a great historical work, but also excellent literary writing.

In the periods that followed, especially the Six Dynasties (Wei, Jin, Song, Qi, Liang and Chen), there was a new trend in prose: many writers paid more attention to form than content. They used very ornate and artificial language, with many balanced sentences. Such works are usually poor in content, for they express few serious or important ideas. At the beginning of the Tang Dynasty, prose of this kind was still written by many people, though a few writers had begun to criticize it.

It was Han Yu and Liu Zongyuan who started a movement to change this prose style, and they succeeded in changing it. Han Yu (768–824) was born in Heyang, Henan. After passing the imperial examinations, he was made an official in the government. He was a philosopher, a poet, and a prose writer.

Portrait of Han Yu

In prose writing, he aimed at reviving the ancient prose style, or the style of the writers before the Han and of the early Han period. According to him, one writes to express one's correct views, "Writing is the vehicle of the Way," as he put it. This means that content is more important than form. He urged writers to use their own language and throw away

Portrait of Liu Zongyuan

phrases and expressions that were no longer fresh. He practised all these principles himself and wrote many powerful and beautiful essays. He was generally regarded as the most outstanding prose writer after Sima Qian.

Liu Zongyuan (773–819) was born in Yongji, Shanxi. Like Han Yu, he became an official after passing the imperial examination. Because of his political views, he was sent to Liuzhou in Guangxi, then a poor and backward area, and died there when he was only 47 years old. He played an active part in the Literary Reform Movement led by Han Yu, and wrote many excellent essays, including fables, short biographies, and impressions of beautiful scenic places.

Together with Han and Liu and after them many of their friends and students who shared their views on writing, wrote in the way they wrote. As a result, the ancient prose style replaced the ornate style of the Six Dynasties and became a new trend. This style was adopted by most writers during later ages until the May Fourth Movement in 1919, when plain spoken Chinese began to be used in writing.

In ancient times there were interesting myths, fables and legends recorded in various philosophical and historical works, such as the *Zuo Zhuan*, the *Zhuang Zi*, the *Han Fei Zi*, the *Records of the Grand Historian*, and the *Mountain and Sea Classic*. These myths and fables are very short and simple; they were written mainly to praise legendary heroes or convey philosophical messages.

Mountain and Sea Classic (Illustration)

The term *xiaoshuo* (small talk) was first seen in a section on authors and books in the *Zhuang Zi*. It may be said that Chinese fiction had its beginnings in the Wei and Jin period. Many stories written during that period can still be found today in anthologies and books, but these stories mainly describe spirits, ghosts, gods and goddesses—a reflection of people's belief in immortals and the supernatural. Interesting and meaningful anecdotes were also written during this period. Many of them are collected in *New Sayings of the World* compiled by Liu Yiqing (403–444).

During the Tang Dynasty there was a remarkable development of ficiton. Many writers not only took a new interest in, but also adopted a new attitude towards the writing of fiction. Before the Tang period, as its name suggested, *xiaoshuo* was an unimportant type of writing, generally looked down upon by serious writers. From the middle period of the Tang Dynasty, quite a few famous writers began to write stories, which were then called *chuanqi* (legend). In form these stories have several new features: they are much longer than those written earlier, and each has a plot, characters, dialogues, and descriptions of people and scenes. They are usually written in very beautiful classical prose. What is more important is that many of them describe real life and therefore reflect social conditions.

Several factors quickened the development of fiction in this period. As a result of economic growth, cities became prosperous, and people of the cities needed amusements and interesting things to read. Life in the cities was a rich source of material for stories. Earlier stories, especially those of the Wei and Jin, though limited in scope, were helpful to the Tang story-tellers, who could draw on the experience shown in those stories. The literary reform started by Han Yu and Liu Zongyuan was helpful, too, because it gave the writers a freer style in which to tell their stories.

Some of the Tang stories are satirical: they reveal the selfish ambitions of those young scholars who were after fame and position. Some stories describe love affairs between young scholars and pretty women, who may be daughters of rich families or prostitutes. There are stories based on historical facts and stories about brave warriors who protect the poor and weak or fight for justice. Some stories expose feudal oppression or sing the praises of true love between men and women.

A still of the Yueju opera "The Story of Li Wa"

As an example, here is the plot of "The Story of Li Wa," which was written by Bai Xingjian, the well-known poet Bai Juyi's brother. A young scholar named Zheng goes to the capital to take part in the imperial examination. He falls in love with a prostitute called Li Wa. When he has spent all his money, the procuress who owns the brothel drives him out. Finding no way to earn a living, he has to work as a singer for an undertaker. While doing his job one day, he is discovered by his father, governor of a prefecture. Considering the son a disgrace to the family, the father gives him a beating and disowns him. Then the young scholar becomes a beggar on the street. On a snowy day, cold and hungry, he cries for help, and happens to be heard by Li Wa. Disregarding the opposition of the procuress, she brings him into her house while saying, "It is my fault that you have suffered so greatly." She does everything she can for him, restores his health, and encourages him to study. After he succeeds in the examinations, he is made a high-ranking official. At this time Li Wa insists on leaving him so that he can marry a lady from an upper-class family. But the scholar decides to marry her, and from then on they live happily together.

Clearly the story praises Li Wa, a woman true to the man she loves. Though a prostitute, she has a sound moral quality, as she is entirely selfless when she looks after the poor, sick and homeless young scholar. The story also reveals an ordinary woman's wish to be able to love the person she really loves.

In later times, writers continued to write short stories in

Romance of the Western Chamber (part), by Qiu Ying of the Ming Dynasty, imitation in the Qing Dynasty

literary classical Chinese. *Strange Stories from a Scholar's Studio*, for instance, is a wonderful work of this type. Besides, many of the Tang stories were later turned into plays. One example is the *Romance of the Western Chamber*, which is based on a short story written by the Tang poet Yuan Zhen. In short, Tang fiction was to have an important influence on later literature.

12

Wang Anshi, Sima Guang and Su Shi: Three Great Figures of the Northern Song Dynasty

Tang's rule was greatly weakened by An Lushan's rebellion (755–763). After him several other regional commanders and border tribes rebelled against the central government, and local wars occurred one after another. Many of the late Tang emperors trusted only their eunuchs, who practically controlled the government and the army. Corruption and internal power struggle led to the cruel oppression of the people. Again, peasant uprisings broke out.

In 875 a man called Huang Chao and his followers started a large-scale peasant uprising in Shandong. Huang had sat for the imperial examination but failed to pass it. He denounced the crimes of the Tang rulers in a declaration after he began to fight. His army took city after city. From Shandong they entered Central China, then East China, and then South China. After a short rest there, they turned north and fought in Hunan, Zhejiang, Anhui and Henan. In 881 they occupied Chang'an. The Tang emperor had fled to Sichuan. Huang declared himself emperor of Daqi.

In 883 Huang had to leave Chang'an, for he was surrounded by Tang troops and his own men were not united. After suffering many defeats in Henan, he finally committed suicide in Shandong, where he had started the uprising.

Portrait of Zhu Wen

Zhu Wen, who had been a general under Huang Chao and later surrendered to the Tang government, became very powerful in Henan. He entered Chang'an in 907, put an end to the Tang Dynasty, and founded the Later Liang. This was the beginning of the period of the Five Dynasties.

The Liang (907–923) was followed by the Tang (923–936), Jin (936–947), Han (947–950) and Zhou (951–960). The capital of the Tang was Luoyang; that of the other four was Kaifeng—an indication of the eastward movement of the political, economic and cultural center of China.

These five dynasties ruled only North China. The south was divided by nine states, and there was another state in Shanxi. These were the Ten States. Many of them lasted longer than the five dynasties put together.

In 960, Zhao Kuangyin, army commander of the Zhou, seized power and founded the Song Dynasty. From 963 to 979 the Song conquered the Ten States one by one and unified China.

Portrait of Zhao Kuangyin

Before this the Khitan tribe had become strong in the Northeast. Shi Jingtang, founder of the Jin of the Five Dynasties, had given 16 prefectures in North China to the Khitan in exchange for their support in his attempt to seize power. Then the Khitan entered North China and called their state Liao.

In the Northwest the Dangxiang tribe founded a state called Western Xia. Liao and Western Xia often attacked Song areas and were a constant threat to the Song.

The Song rulers studied the causes of the fall of the Tang and came to the conclusion that military commanders of the Tang had been too powerful and independent to be controlled by the emperors. So during the Song period the commanders were given only limited power and lower positions than important civilian officials. Scholars were more respected than warriors. The economy developed, culture flourished, but national defence was weak.

North and east of the state of Liao was the area where the Nvzhen tribes lived. At first the Liao rulers tried to control them. Later, the Nvzhen grew stronger and stronger, and in 1125 they conquered Liao and established a state called Jin. In 1127 the Jin troops attacked Kaifeng, the capital of the Song, and took it. That was the end of the Northern Song.

One of the sons of Huizong, the last emperor of the Northern Song, was not captured by the Jin troops. He was made the emperor of the Southern Song in 1127.

Portrait of Wang Anshi

Wang Anshi (1021–1086) was born into an ordinary landlord family in Linchuan, Jiangxi. After passing the imperial examinations, he was an official in local governments for many years. This experience gave him a good opportunity to understand the social ills and the hardships and wishes of the ordinary people. In 1058 he wrote a memorial to the emperor suggesting a reform, but the emperor turned a deaf ear to his proposals. Then a new emperor came to the throne. He saw some of the problems of the country and decided to use the famous Wang Anshi and empower him to carry out reforms.

From 1069 Wang and a few other officials enforced new laws for about 15 years. They aimed at encouraging agricultural production by reducing the burdens of the common people and also by carrying out projects helpful to the development of agriculture. At the same time, the new laws limited the privileges of high-ranking officials and big landlords, who naturally hated Wang's reform. The result of the reform was quite good: the economy grew and the revenue of the government increased. As it was opposed by powerful people, it was stopped after the emperor who had favored it died. This was the greatest social reform of the whole feudal period of our country.

Wang Anshi was also a poet and philosopher. Many of his views were very progressive in his day. He said, for instance, that Heaven had neither will nor feelings, and therefore could not react to man's good or evil conduct, or favor or oppose anything man did. Heaven and earth, he said, move and change of themselves and are independent of man's will or feelings.

According to him, the universe is made up of the five elements (metal, wood, water, fire and earth). These five elements are moving and changing because within each of them are two forces, two materials, two qualities, etc. One is soft and the other is hard; one is bright and the other is dark, one beautiful and the other ugly; one good and the other evil, etc. This view is very similar to the modern concept of the unity of opposites.

Wang knew that nature has its own laws, which cannot be changed. It is possible for man to know the laws of nature, if man observes and studies. One should look and listen before one can think. He wrote a short essay with the title of "The Sad Story of Zhongyong." Zhongyong is an unusual child who can read and write before he is taught by anyone. His father often takes him to the homes of rich or important people to show off his genius, but neglects his education. As a result, after he grows up, Zhongyong is no different from any other man. The story points out clearly that one has to learn to acquire knowledge.

His best-known saying is, "The will of Heaven need not be feared; ancestors need not be followed; and other people's words need not be worried about."

Sima Qian of the Western Han Dynasty was the first historian who wrote a general history from the earliest times to his own day. In the Northern Song period, a historian also called Sima wrote another general history that covers the long period from the early Warring States Period to the end of the Five Dynasties. This great work is *Zi Zhi Tong Jian*, or *Mirror of History*. Its author is Sima Guang.

Sima Guang (1019–1086) was born in Xiaxian, Shanxi. After passing the imperial examinations and becoming an official in the central government, he made up his mind to compile a general history which could be studied by emperors and ministers and would help them to learn from history and rule with wisdom and foresight. He chose the form of chronicle, in which important events that happened in the same year are grouped together.

The whole work consists of 294 volumes. Its record of history starts from the year 403 BC and stops at 959, so altogether the events of 1,362 years are included. Its material comes from 17 authorized historical works, and all kinds of unauthorized histories, biographies, and various collections of literary works.

Sima Guang and his three colleagues worked on it for 19 years. Politically Sima Guang was very conservative. He was opposed to Wang Anshi's reforms. When Wang was dismissed from the central government, he was made the chief minister, and he stopped all the new laws that Wang had started. But in compiling his great historical work, he adopted a generally objective attitude. Just like Sima Qian's *Record of the Grand Historian*, the *Mirror of History* was read and studied almost by all government officials and scholars.

After Sima Guang some other historians also wrote general histories in the form of chronicle.

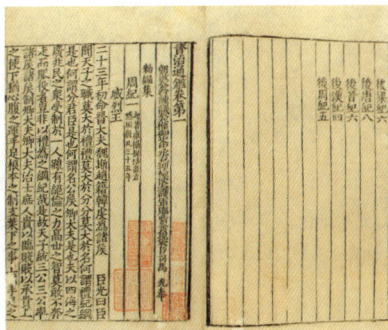

Mirror of History

Su Shi (1037–1101) was born in Meishan, Sichuan. His father Su Xun and his younger brother Su Zhe were both well-known essayists, and the three of them were among the "eight prose masters of the Tang and Song periods." He passed the imperial examinations at 21 and became a local official. When Wang Anshi was implementing his reform, Su was in the capital. A conservative in his political views, Su was opposed to Wang's reform, and for this reason he asked to be sent away from the capital. He worked in Hangzhou, Suzhou, and other cities for a few years, and was once imprisoned by the reformists.

Portrait of Su Shi

After Sima Guang began to lead the government and Wang Anshi's reform was reversed, Su Shi was summoned to the capital and assigned to various posts in the central government. But by this time his views had changed. Having seen some of the advantages of reform, he wrote

Sansuyuan Scenic Spot, Pingdingshan City, Henan Province

memorials to the emperor saying that Wang's new laws had certain good points and therefore should not be abolished altogether. This made the conservatives in power dislike him and send him out of the capital. Later, the reformists won power again, and took revenge on the conservatives. Su Shi could not escape his misfortunes. He was more than once demoted and sent to Danzhou in distant Hainan Island. He was finally pardoned by the new emperor and allowed to return north. In the next year he died in Changzhou, Jiangsu, when he was 64.

In the struggle between the reformists and the conservatives Su Shi wavered and was liked by neither side. Traditional education made him conservative in thinking, but his experiences as a local official helped him to understand some of the beneficial effects of reform. This conflict led to his tragic fate.

In sharp contrast to his political disappointments, he had brilliant achievements in literature, and could be regarded as the most influential writer of the Northern Song period. He wrote over 2,700 poems and over 300 lyrics in the form of *ci*, and many articles and essays. In his works force and elegance, grandeur and delicacy, straightforwardness and subtlety, are admirably combined. People said that his prose and poetry were natural like floating clouds and flowing water, which go forward when they should go forward, and stop when they ought to stop.

His literary works reflect different aspects of his thinking. There are poems showing his sympathy with the common working people, his enjoyment of nature, his dissatisfaction with the political situation, and his dreams of leading an unrestrained life free from the tedious requirements of custom he had to observe as an official. Traces of Confucian, Buddhist and Taoist ideas can all be found in his works.

Life today is no longer worth painting;
County officials knock at doors at night
To demand payment of taxes.

而今风物那堪画，县吏催钱夜打门。

Li children with their hair tied like horns,
Blow onion leaves to meet their elders.

总角黎家三四童，口吹葱叶送迎翁。

I wish to compare the West Lake to Xi Shi, like her
It is always beautiful, with light or heavy make up.

欲把西湖比西子，淡妆浓抹总相宜。

A spring view at the West Lake

> *The cool wind on the river produces sound caught by our ears,*
> *and the bright moon in the mountains becomes color seen by our eyes.*
> *We are always free to have them and enjoy them,*
> *for there is no end to them. They are the Creator's inexhaustible treasury, which you and I can share.*

唯江上之清风，与山间之明月，耳得之而为声，目遇之而成色，取之无禁，用之不竭，是造物者之无尽藏也，而吾与子之所共适。

Su Shi's valuable contributions to the development of *ci* will be discussed in Chapter 14.

13

Zhu Xi:
The Synthesizer of the
Philosophy of Principle

As has been mentioned, Buddhism and Taoism, and what was called "mysterious learning" were popular among intellectuals during the Wei and Jin and the period of the Southern and Northern Dynasties. After this period of division there was the Sui Dynasty, which lasted only 37 years before it was replaced by the Tang. Many Tang official-scholars including the famous Han Yu and Li Ao were determined to restore the authority of Confucianism by attacking Buddhism and Taoism. This effort was continued during the Northern Song by important scholars like Ouyang Xiu and Fan Zhongyan. After them, there emerged a number of outstanding philosophers, among whom were Zhou Dunyi, Shao Yong, Zhang Zai, Cheng Hao and Cheng Yi. They explored a series of fundamental problems regarding the universe and human life, such as principle (*li*) and material-force (*qi*), the Way (*dao*) and the instrument (*qi*), *yin* and *yang*, human nature and human feelings, principle (*li*) and desire, knowledge and practice, etc. Discussions of these categories showed that they were concerned with more and newer questions than earlier philosophers. The philosophy of this period, generally called the philosophy of principle, was indeed more systematic, more speculative, more subtle, larger in scope, and richer in content than earlier philosophy. Its core was certainly Confucianism, but it contained some Buddhist and Taoist elements.

In the Southern Song, the philosophy of principle was further developed. With Zhu Xi this philosophy reached its climax and completion. Zhu may be regarded as the synthesizer not only of the philosophy of principle, but of Chinese philosophy from Dong Zhongshu to his day.

Zhu Xi (1130–1200) was born into a scholar's family in Wuyuan, Jiangxi. When young, he made an extensive study of

Confucianism, Buddhism, especially Zen Buddhism, and Taoism. He also studied history and literature. He was truly a learned scholar with a profound knowledge in many fields. After he passed the imperial examinations, he was a government official for some time, but he spent the greater part of his life as a teacher and author. He compiled a number of books ,the most

Portrait of Zhu Xi

popular being the *Four Books*, comprising *The Analects*, *The Book of Mencius*, *The Great Learning*, and *The Doctrine of the Mean*. These four books and the notes and commentaries he wrote for them were to become standard textbooks studied by all scholars who intended to sit for the imperial examinations in later dynasties. His conversations with his students on various philosophical topics were recorded and edited, and made up a huge book called *Classified Conversations of Zhu Zi*.

Below are some of the main points he discussed:

Principle and material-force. Following the Cheng brothers (Cheng Hao and Cheng Yi), Zhu Xi held that the principle was the origin of the universe. In other words, there was first the principle and then there was the universe and all the things in it. But principle and material-force cannot be separated. There is no material-force without principle, nor is there principle without material-force. Before there was a chair, he said, the principle of the chair was already there. A chair has to have four legs—that is something determined by the principle.

There are countless things in the world. Does it follow that there are countless principles? Zhu Xi said that there is only one

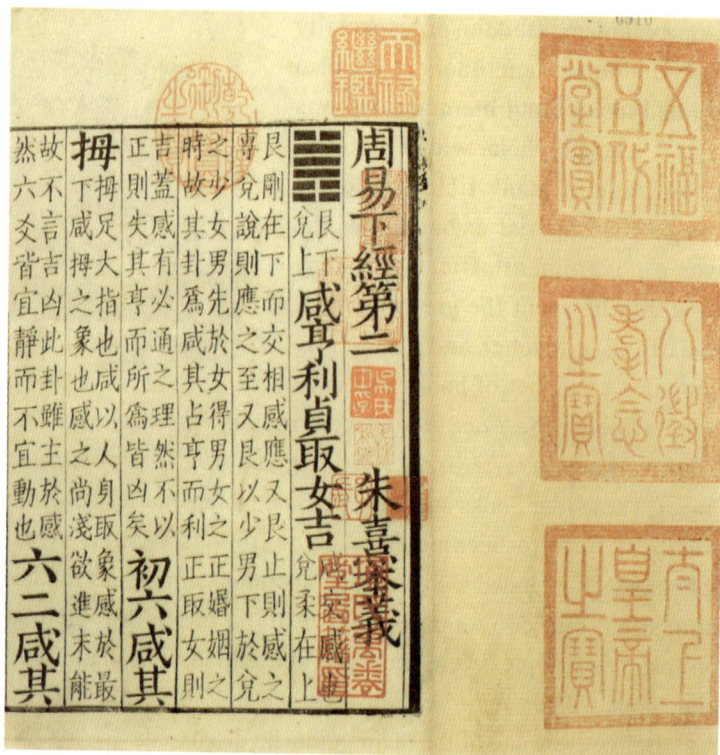

Original Meaning of the Book of Changes by Zhu Xi

original principle—the Supreme Ultimate. The countless principles embodied in countless things are all derived from this original principle. This is comparable to the fact that there is only one moon in the sky, but in ten thousand rivers and lakes there are its reflections.

But Zhang Zai and some other philosophers of the time had a different view. They said that material-force is the basis of existence. It is eternal, boundless, present everywhere at any time. Principle is an attribute of material-force. It exists not before, but within material-force.

Human nature. According to Zhu and some other Song philosophers, human nature is principle embodied in human beings. It is good, pure and virtuous. But not every person is virtuous. The reason is that human beings are made of different types of material-force, and this difference makes them different in moral qualities. Sages are endowed with pure material-force; so their nature is like a pearl in clear water. Evil people are endowed with dirty material-force, and their nature is like a pearl in muddy water. In short, human nature as a reflection of principle is good, but personal qualities affected by material-force may be evil.

Heavenly principle and selfish desire. According to Zhu and other philosophers of the school of principle, human nature corresponds to heavenly principle, and it finds expression in the four virtues of humanity, rightness, propriety and wisdom, and the ethical code that governs the relations between father and son, brother and brother, and husband and wife. But human desire may be bad, selfish and dangerous. Therefore Zhu Xi called on people to "keep heavenly principle and get rid of selfish desire."

So the ruler should be virtuous and just, and the common people should be obedient, law-abiding and uphold the ethical code. All people should behave according to the heavenly principle, which has never changed and will never change. But Zhu Xi did not say who was to ensure that the ruler behaved according to heavenly principle and removed selfish desires.

The necessity of examining concrete objects. Zhu Xi said that to understand the principle one should examine its manifestations in concrete objects. The more objects one examines, the wider one's knowledge will be. This is a process of the accumulation of knowledge, and the result will be the thorough understanding of the principle, or enlightenment. Based on *The Doctrine of the Mean*, he held that the correct study method should be to "learn extensively, inquire carefully, think deeply, differentiate clearly and practise faithfully."

According to Zhu Xi, not only nature, but also human society, was governed or guided by the principle, which was eternal. It is clear that he believed that the feudal system would not change and could not be changed. For this reason, in the dynasties after the Song his philosophy was highly acclaimed. His influence was once spread to Japan, Korea and other East Asian countries.

14

Ci-Poems
in Irregular Meter

Ci is a variety of poetry. It is different from ordinary poetry in that its lines are not of the same length, while each line of a poem has a fixed number of words, generally five or seven words. However, the number of lines and the number of words in each line of *ci* are not flexible, neither are its tonal pattern and rhyme scheme. There are fixed tunes or forms, and poets have to write *ci* according to them, or fill them with proper words.

It was said that originally this form of poetry was created and adopted by musicians and singers among the ordinary people. *Ci* means words of songs. Later it was used by poets, who gradually made it very literary.

Among the earliest *ci* writers were Li Bai and Bai Juyi, the two famous Tang poets. Some other Tang poets also used this form. They mainly wrote about personal feelings, especially feelings of women. Their *ci* works are very beautiful, but usually poor in content.

Li Yu (937–978), the last emperor of the Southern Tang (one of the Ten States), was the most remarkable *ci* writer of the period of the Five Dynasties. Although a talented poet, he was a poor ruler. His state was conquered by the Song, and he was taken to Bianjing (now Kaifeng) as a prisoner. In his *ci* works he wrote about the old happy days when he was an

Portrait of Li Yu

emperor, his sadness at losing his kingdom, and the women he had loved. His works are full of beautiful imagery and imagination, and they are widely read and liked. Here is one:

Silent and alone, I go up the stairs of the western chamber.
The moon is like a hook.
With a lonely tree the deep courtyard locks in the clear
autumn.
It cannot be cut apart with scissors,
Nor can it be disentangled,
For it is the sadness of departure;
In the heart it has an indescribable taste.

无言独上西楼，月如钩。寂寞梧桐深院锁清秋。剪
不断，理还乱，是离愁，别是一番滋味在心头。

During the Song period, *ci* prospered. It became more popular, more refined and more colorful than it had been before. Besides poets, emperors and ministers, actresses and prostitutes, also tried to write it. There were over 200 Song poets whose *ci* works were later collected and preserved, and they used as many as 870 different tunes.

From the late Tang to the early Song, the themes of *ci* were generally confined to personal joys and sorrows, and to love between men and women. Liu Yong (984?–1053?), a very popular *ci* writer, had a wider range of themes. Many of his works describe urban scenes, the life of actresses and prostitutes, and the feelings of lonely travellers.

It was Su Shi who brought about a change in the style of *ci*. His *ci* works not only describe departure and friendship, but praise ancient heroes, express his own patriotic sentiments and heroic aspirations, show his sympathy with the poor and his wish to become one with nature. The range of his topics is much wider than that of any other *ci* writer. Most poets before him wrote *ci* in a delicate and refined style. He started a heroic and vigorous style, and opened a new path for the development of this literary form. Here is the first half of his well-known *ci* on the history of *Chibi* (Red Cliffs):

Chibi

The great river flows eastward;
Its waves have swept away all the ancient heroes.
West of the old fortress,
People say, is Red Cliff where Lord Zhou fought during the
time of the Three Kingdoms.
The jagged rocks thrust into the air;
The wild waves dash upon the shore,
And roll up a thousand heaps of snow.
The river and mountain form a beautiful picture,
Reminding people of the many heroes there once were!

　　大江东去，浪淘尽，千古风流人物。故垒西边，人道是，三国周郎赤壁。乱石穿空，惊涛拍岸，卷起千堆雪。江山如画，一时多少豪杰。

A few years before Su Shi died, a woman poet of unusual talent was born in Shandong. Her name was Li Qingzhao (1084–1155?). Before the collapse of the Northern Song, she and her husband Zhao Mingcheng led a happy life. Shortly after they fled south to escape the Jin troops, Zhao died. She wandered alone in the southeast for the rest of her life.

Portrait of Li Qingzhao

She wrote beautiful poems, *ci* and prose, but was mainly known for her *ci*. Those she wrote before she fled south describe her life as a young girl and a young wife, and express her love of nature. There was a clear change in her style after she went south. Then she wrote about her misfortunes, which also reflect the misfortunes of the country. In her day it was very difficult for a woman to become a learned person, let alone a poet. She was brave enough to break through the limitations that feudal customs imposed on women and choose her own way of life.

Here is one of her best-known short *ci* works:

Last night the rain was weak but the wind was fierce;
After a deep sleep the effects of wine still remain.
I ask the maid as she is rolling up the screen,
And she says, "No change in the crabapple tree."
Don't you know,
Don't you know,
There should be more green but less red.

昨夜雨疏风骤，浓睡不消残酒。试问卷帘人，却道海棠依旧。知否？知否？应是绿肥红瘦。

Portrait of Lu You

The Southern Song produced two famous poets: Lu You and Xin Qiji.

Lu You (1125–1210) was born in Shaoxing, Zhejiang. His father and his father's friends were patriotic scholars, and their influence cultivated in the boy a deep love for his country and his people. He loved to study and studied hard when he was young, and was known as a poet when he was not yet 20. At 29 he passed the imperial examinations, but he was not given a government post because he was disliked by those in power. At that time the emperor and many important ministers followed an appeasement policy, and did not want to fight the Jin, which had occupied North and Central China, but Lu You was opposed to this policy.

After serving in the army stationed in Sichuan for a few years, he worked as an unimportant official in Fujian, Jiangxi and Zhejiang. Finally, at 66, he returned to his hometown, where he lived most of the time during the rest of his life. He died when he was an old man of 85 with the bitter disappointment that he had not seen North and Central China recovered from the enemy.

He left behind as many as over 9,000 poems, many of which are full of patriotic feelings and militant spirit. He also wrote poems describing the life and miseries of the ordinary people. In painting a truthful picture of his age he is like Du Fu, and in the use of language he seems to have been influenced by Bai Juyi, for he uses very simple and natural language.

He wrote about 130 *ci* works. In his *ci* works he talks about the fate of his country, and his own disappointment at the political and military situation, like the following lines:

The enemy has not yet been defeated,
But my hair is turning grey.
My tears have flowed in vain.
Never did I expect
Although my heart is on the Tianshan Mountains,
I am growing old in a quiet place by a river.

胡未灭，鬓先秋，泪空流。此生谁料，心在天山，身老沧洲。

Here "the Tianshan Mountains" refer to the front. The last two lines express his deep sorrow at being unable to carry out his wishes.

Xin Qiji (1140–1207) was born in Jinan, Shandong. When the Jin troops were sweeping south against the Southern Song, he joined those people who had armed themselves to fight the invaders. Later he crossed the Yangtze River to work for the Southern Song government. In spite of his low position, he wrote to the emperor, putting forward suggestions about resistance.

Portrait of Xin Qiji

The Southern Song rulers, following the policy of nonresistance, never gave him any important post or an opportunity to fight the enemy. He died at 68 with his cherished dreams unfulfilled.

Most of his literary works are *ci*, over 600 of which have been collected. He carried forward the heroic and bold style that Su Shi had started. His works are very colorful and rich in content, reflecting from different angles the social life of his day and his own feelings. He has been regarded as the most outstanding patriotic *ci* writer of the Southern Song period.

Where can I see the Central Plains?
Around Beigu Tower the scenery is very beautiful.
How many states have risen and fallen in the past thousand years!
They are endless,
Just like the endless Yangtze River rolling on.

何处望神州？满眼风光北固楼。千古兴亡多少事？悠悠，不尽长江滚滚流。

These are the first few lines of the well-known *ci* "To the Tune of Nanxiangzi: Thoughts on Ascending Beigu Tower near Jingkou." In it the poet expresses his view on history and reveals his concern for his country.

Xin Qiji's *ci* and Lu You's poems encouraged the people of the Southern Song to fight the enemy and win victories in the war. In later ages, whenever there was a national crisis, people would turn to these two great patriotic poets, and draw courage and inspiration from their works.

15

The Four Great Inventions

During the Song period the Chinese people further developed the making of the compass, paper, gunpowder and the art of printing. Together, they are called the four great inventions that China contributed to the world.

As early as the Warring States period the magnetic force of magnet was discovered, and a sort of instrument was made of magnet to show directions. This was certainly the earliest compass in the world. What it was like is unknown today.

During the Han period, people made a spoon-like compass. A small spoon, made of magnet, with a very smooth bottom, was placed on a square copper plate. The center of the plate was ground smooth to make it easy for the spoon to move. When the spoon, after it was turned, came to a stop, its handle would point to the south.

This form of compass was further improved during the Song period. People made iron needles and rubbed them on a piece of magnet, so that they would become magnetic. Then one such needle was hung with a thin thread, or put on something light that floated on the water in a bowl. The latter was the compass that was first used in navigation.

Portrait of Cai Lun

China was the first country in the world to use the compass on sea-going ships. Historical records show that in 1099–1102 the compass was used on ships sailing to and from Guangzhou.

It was generally believed that paper was first made by a man called Cai Lun in 105 during the Eastern Han Dynasty. However, in recent decades, earlier paper made during the Western Han was unearthed in Xinjiang, Shanxi and Gansu. So we have reason to believe that paper was invented in the Western Han and was improved by Cai Lun in the Eastern Han. In later periods, different materials were used for making paper, and its quality became better and

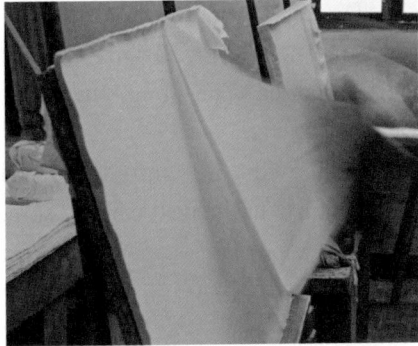

Xuan paper in production

better. The famous Xuan paper, produced in Xuanzhou, Anhui, first appeared in the Tang Dynasty. Its quality was so good that all calligraphers and painters liked to use it. Even today it is considered the best kind of paper for calligraphy and traditional Chinese painting.

During the Song period, bamboo began to be used for making paper, and the output of bamboo paper increased rapidly.

In 751, during the reign of Tang Xuanzong, the Chinese technique of paper-making was introduced to the Arab world, and from there to Europe in 1150. In other words, Europe knew how to make paper about a thousand years later than China.

The Chinese invented gunpowder over 1,100 years ago. Towards the end of the Tang, gunpowder was first used in war. In 904, during a battle between local forces, a weapon then called "flying fire" was used. It was a packet of gunpowder tied to the head of an arrow. After the fuse was lighted, the arrow was shot to the enemy side, and the gunpowder would cause damage or kill men.

During the Song period, the making and use of gunpowder reached a new level. Various kinds of weapons with gunpowder were invented. The Song, Jin and Yuan armies all used these weapons in war.

Gunpowder was introduced to the Arab world during the 13th century. In the next century some European countries began to make gunpowder weapons with methods they had learned from the Arabs.

Huolong Chu Shui (Fire dragon coming out of the water), an ancient weapon

Before printing was invented, people had to rely on handwriting to reproduce a book. It was very slow and errors easily occurred.

Woodblock printing first appeared in the early Tang period. It was developed from the use of seals and stone engraving. Words engraved on stones could last very long, and later, in about the 4th century, the method of rubbing a piece of paper on an engraved stone covered with ink was used to make copies. This gave workers the idea of engraving words on a woodblock and printing them. With the quick development of the economy and culture in the Tang Dynasty, books and other publications like calendars were needed by the public, and this demanded promoted woodblock printing. According to records in certain books, block printing was very common in the late Tang period.

During the Song Dynasty, the technique of block printing was very advanced. Books were beautifully printed. Even today the books printed at that time are valuable and treasured by libraries and book collectors.

Woodblock printing

Block printing was not very convenient. Every two pages of a book had to be engraved on a wood block, and a big book would require many blocks. Besides, there had to be large places for storing the blocks. To overcome these shortcomings, Bi Sheng invented the movable type during the years between 1041 and 1048. One word was carved on one piece of clay, which was hardened with fire. Then clay characters were set on an iron plate according to the text of a book. Then ink was applied to them and sheets of paper spread over them, and the printing was done.

Bi Sheng's invention made printing faster and easier than before. Later, movable type of metal and wood was made and widely used. One county magistrate of the Yuan period had over 30,000 wood characters carved, with which he printed a book he had written. It was a book of more than 60,000 characters, and he finished printing 600 copies in less than a month.

The technique of printing was gradually known to other Asian countries and Europe. The great influence printing had on the advance of civilization is too clear to need any explanation.

After its founding in 1127, the Southern Song was under the constant threat of the Jin in the north. The people and many patriotic generals like Yue Fei wanted to fight against the Jin and recover the lost land, but most emperors and important ministers would rather accept the harsh and insulting conditions imposed by the Jin than resist and attack the enemy. It was clearly their first concern to maintain the shaky existence of the dynasty in the south.

In 1234 the Jin was conquered by the Mongols, who less than 50 years later, occupied south China and put an end to Song rule.

During the 11th and 12th centuries, there were many nomadic tribes living on the grassland of what is Mongolia today. The Mongols, one of those tribes, had a great leader who was later called Genghis Khan (1162–1227). He unified all the tribes on the grassland through a series of battles, and founded the Mongolian state. When he had made his rule stable, Genghis Khan started aggressive wars against his neighbors. In three westward

Portrait of Genghis Khan

expeditions, he and his sons occupied North China, Central Asia, Eastern Europe (including part of Russia, Poland and Hungary), and part of the Middle East. The empire was too large to be ruled by one government, so it was divided into four parts called khanates, each ruled by one of Genghis Khan's sons or grandsons.

Shortly after the Mongols conquered the Jin (1234), they started attacking the Southern Song. Everywhere the Song army and people put up indomitable resistance; the Mongols advanced very slowly and suffered heavy losses. The Great Khan (Genghis

Khan's grandson) who personally directed the invasion in Sichuan was killed in a battle. Unfortunately the Song rulers were bent on reaching an agreement with the enemy and therefore would not give proper support to the front. In 1276 the Mongols occupied Hangzhou, the capital of the Southern Song. It came to an end three years later. Eight years before, in 1271, Kublai Khan had founded the Yuan Dynasty and made Beijing its capital.

The political and economic systems of the Yuan were basically those of the former dynasties, but Han people, were discriminated against and oppressed. They were excluded from important positions both in the government and in the army. The imperial examinations were stopped. Because of this, Han scholars were unable to become officials.

As the Mongols ruled over the greater part of Asia and part of Europe, communications between these two continents were made easier than before. Groups of people from Europe and the Middle East came to China. Among them was the well-known traveller Marco Polo (1254–1324) from the city of Venice in present-day Italy.

16

Yuan Drama: One of the Three Peaks in the History of Drama in the World

When people talk about Chinese literature, they often mention three literary forms and their three golden ages: Tang poem, Song *ci*, and Yuan *qu*.

Yuan *qu* refers to two different types of writing: *sanqu* and *zaju*. The former, like *ci*, is a form of poetry. There are fixed tunes, and poets compose words for them. Its language is generally more colloquial than that of *ci*. In style it is more direct, passionate and forceful.

The rise of *sanqu* was connected with the new political and social conditions in North China. Border tribes including the Khitan, the Nvzhen and the Mongols moved into North China, bringing with them their music played on horseback. When this music was merged with the passionate songs of Hebei and Liaodong, *sanqu* was born. So *sanqu* came from the ordinary people; only later did poets write in this form. That was why it was looked down upon by scholars at first, and not many *sanqu* compositions were left behind. Today only about 4,000 of them can be found in various anthologies. The number is much smaller than the nearly 50,000 Tang poems and 20,000 Song *ci* that have been collected.

Among the best-known *sanqu* compositions is "Autumn Thoughts" by Ma Zhiyuan:

A withered vine, an old tree, and a dazed crow;
A small bridge, a flowing stream, and a cottage;
An ancient road, a west wind, and a lean horse.
The sun setting in the west,
And a man with a broken heart in the remotest place.

　　枯藤老树昏鸦，小桥流水人家，古道西风瘦马，夕阳西下，断肠人在天涯。

　　This *sanqu* is mainly made up of a series of nouns and their modifiers. Together they present a picture of a lonely, sad traveller in a desolate strange place far from home, not knowing what is waiting for him and not sure of his own future.

　　Sanqu is different from but connected with *zaju*, which means drama. *Sanqu* can be read and sung, but cannot be acted. *Zaju* is written for the stage; it is complete with a plot, dialogues, songs and stage directions. The songs in *zaju* are in the form of *sanqu*.

　　During the Yuan period *zaju*, or drama, prospered. There were about 100 dramatists who wrote about 500 plays, but most of them were unfortunately lost long ago.

There were several factors that made it possible for drama to develop in this period. Cities grew as a result of the growth of handicrafts and commerce, and people living in cities needed recreation and amusements. It was then possible for singers, story-tellers, actors and actresses to make a living. Scholars and writers who had frowned upon drama were then interested in it, and began to write it, because they wanted to use it as a weapon for attacking the rule they hated. Besides, in the early period of the Yuan Dynasty, imperial examinations were stopped, and Han scholars were no longer able to get government posts, as they were discriminated against. They had to live as and among the ordinary people, and therefore they had a good understanding of the ordinary people's life and feelings, which gave them rich material for their plays.

The first well-known Yuan dramatist that should be mentioned is Guan Hanqing. He lived in the 13th century; the dates of his birth and death are uncertain. A native of Dadu (now Beijing), he worked there as a doctor, but was known for the many plays he wrote. His works include tragedies, comedies and historical plays. Some of them describe the life of the people of his day; others are based on historical events. All of them sing praises of the oppressed or expose the evils of the ruling classes. The characters in his plays are all very vivid, convincing and impressive, and they reveal their personalities in dramatic conflicts.

The *Injustice Suffered by Dou E* may be Guan's best-known tragedy. When Dou E is seven years old, she is given by her father to an old woman to be her son's child bride. Ten years later, they are married. Shortly afterwards the young man dies and Dou E becomes a widow. She stays with her mother-in-law, hoping to live a peaceful life with her. An evil man called Zhang wants to

A still of the Sichuan opera *Injustice Suffered by Dou E*

get hold of Dou E, and is rejected by the young woman. When the mother-in-law falls ill, Zhang prepares some poison, intending to kill the old woman. However, the poison is eaten by Zhang's father by mistake, and the old man dies at once. Then Zhang says to Dou E that he will charge her with the murder of his father if she still refuses to marry him. As she has seen through him, she would rather go to court with him than marry him. Contrary to her expectations, the governor who tries their case is a corrupt official and convicts her without any reason or evidence. He sentences her to death, and this good young woman is killed. But her ghost continues to fight against injustice. When her father comes to the region as a high-ranking official, her ghost appears in his dream and tells him the truth of the case. He then examines the case, corrects the wrong verdict, and punishes the evil Zhang and the governor.

The play praises Dou E's fighting spirit and exposes and condemns the dark society and unjust legal system. In many of

A still of the Kunqu opera *Romance of the Western Chamber*

his plays Guan Hanqing gives truthful pictures of the people's sufferings under Yuan rule. Realism in his plays is intense and powerful.

A little later than and as famous as Guan was the dramatist Wang Shifu. He also lived in Dadu and wrote many palys. The one that made him known in later ages was *Romance of the Western Chamber*, which is based on "Life of Yingying," a short story written by the Tang poet Yuan Zhen.

Yingying is a beautiful young woman living with her mother, Madame Cui, in a temple. A young scholar named Zhang happens to be living in the same temple. He helps to protect Yingying and her mother from an attack by a group of disorderly soldiers. To show her gratitude to the scholar, Madame Cui promises to marry her daughter to him. But soon she goes back on her word, saying that Yingying has been engaged to a high-ranking official's son. With the help of Hongniang, Yingying's maid, the young lady and the scholar secretly meet and spend a lot of happy time together. When Madame Cui hears about this, she has to give her consent to their marriage, but she insists that Zhang should first pass the imperial examinations and get a government post. Zhang succeeds in these two things, and the two lovers are finally united.

There are beautiful songs in this play, as in many others. The one sung by Yingying on the day Zhang leaves for the capital is very popular:

Blue clouds in the sky,
Yellow flowers on the ground,
The west wind is blowing hard,
And the northern wild geese are flying southward.
What in the morning has dyed
The frosty trees red, as if they were drunk?
It must be the tears of those who are to part.

碧云天，黄花地，西风紧，北雁南飞。晓来谁染霜林醉？总是离人泪。

It is clear that the dramatist sympathizes with Zhang and Yingying, who dare to defy feudal traditions and have the courage to fall in love with each other without their parents' permission. On the other hand, he makes Madame Cui appear foolish and insincere in trying to defend old customs.

A still of the dance drama *The Orphan of the Zhao Family*

There are many other famous plays, such as *Autumn in the Han Palace* by Ma Zhiyuan, *Qiannü's Soul Goes Wandering* by Zheng Guangzu, and *Over the Wall and on the Horse* by Bai Pu.

Several Yuan plays were translated into European languages in the 18th and 19th centuries. One of them, *The Orphan of the Zhao Family* by Ji Junxiang, attracted great attention in Europe. It tells an ancient story of revenge. One cruel man in power has killed all the descendants and relatives of his enemy, except one child. To protect him many loyal people sacrifice themselves. The child is saved and takes revenge on the cruel man when he grows up. The play was first translated into French in 1734, and then into other languages. Voltaire, the well-known French writer, historian and philosopher of the 18th century, was deeply moved by the play. He adapted it and changed its name to *The Orphan of China*. In 1755 the play was performed on the stage in Paris. In the preface to the play Voltaire wrote that the play showed that reason and intellect would eventually overcome ignorance and barbarity.

The rise of Yuan drama was about 300 years earlier than the time of Shakespeare and other English dramatists. It may be called the second of the three peaks in the history of drama in the world: ancient Greek and Roman drama, Yuan drama, and English drama of the age of Shakespeare.

17

The Rebuilding of Beijing and Zheng He's Voyages

Towards the end of the Yuan Dyansty, racial oppression, corrupt government, and natural disasters made life difficult for the people. Again, peasant uprisings broke out. One peasant army was led by a man called Liu Futong. To distinguish themselves from other people, the soldiers of this army tied red scarves around their heads, and gradually they were called the "Red Scarf Army." They fought mainly in the Huai River valley, capturing one town after another, and more and more men joined them. For some time they occupied Kaifeng, Henan, and the neighbouring areas. But then they made military and political mistakes, and Liu was forced to withdraw to northern Anhui, where he died in action.

Portrait of Zhu Yuanzhang

Another branch of the Red Scarf Army, led by Guo Zixing, was active in the area around Fengyang, Anhui. Under Guo was a man called Zhu Yuanzhang, who was to found the Ming Dynasty.

Born into a poor peasant's family in Fengyang, Zhu worked as a herdsman for a landlord when he was a boy. His parents and brothers all died in a plague. As there was no one to look after him, he had to enter a Buddhist temple to be a monk. Later, when the temple could not feed him, he left it and became a roaming monk, and managed to live by begging. After Guo Zixing started a revolt against the Yuan, Zhu joined him, and quickly distinguished himself as a brave and capable fighter. Before long he was made a general, and became the commander of the army after Guo died. He had been fighting Yuan troops north of the Yangtze River before he crossed it in 1356 and occupied Nanjing. Then he entered Zhejiang and expanded his base areas.

While Zhu was growing powerful, many scholars from the landlord class came to help him, and he listened to their advice. He began to aspire to found a dynasty, forgetting about the interests of the peasants from whom he had emerged.

After defeating rival rebel leaders, he brought South China under his control. In 1367 he began the northern expedition. His forces first took Shandong, then Henan and Shaanxi. When the greater part of North China was cleared of Yuan troops, his army marched northward and was soon close to Dadu, now Beijing, the capital of the Yuan. The last Yuan emperor fled into the homeland of the Mongols further north, and the Yuan Dynasty came to an end in 1368.

Zhu declared himself the emperor of the new dynasty—the Ming Dynasty—in the same year, and made Nanjing his capital. The whole country was unified in 1387 with the recovery of Liaodong.

In 1398, after being the emperor for 30 years, Zhu Yuanzhang died at the age of 71. His eldest son had died at that time, so the throne was given to his grandson, Zhu Yunwen. But one of the young emperor's uncles, Zhu Di, Zhu Yuanzhang's fourth son, wanted to seize power. Zhu Di had been stationed in Beijing with a huge army. His army fought all the way south and took Nanjing in 1402. Zhu Di ascended the throne and moved the capital to Beijing, which remained the capital of the Ming until the end of the dynasty.

Zhu Di decided to rebuild Beijing. About 250,000 artisans and nearly one million peasants were mobilized for the project. In the center of the city a huge palace was built. Generally called the Forbidden City, the palace covers an area of 720,000 square meters and contains over 9,000 rooms, surrounded by city walls and moats. The three great halls in the front part are magnificent and imposing; there is an air of solemnity and stability about them, symbolizing the power of the emperor. In the back are many courtyards with rooms for the emperor's family and their servants. Repaired or partly rebuilt from time to time, the palace is still complete and in good condition.

This imperial palace is perhaps the largest and grandest of its kind in the world that can be seen today. It embodies the fine tradition of ancient Chinese architecture, and the great wisdom and creativeness of the working people. Now as a museum open to the public, it attracts tens of thousands of visitors from different parts of China and abroad every day.

While Beijing was being rebuilt, the Grand Canal, which

A full view of the Forbidden City

links the capital to the lower reaches of the Yangtze River, was dredged. Food grain, silk and cotton cloth produced in the south were shipped along this river to the north.

Zhu Di and his successor sent Zheng He, who was working in their palace, as an envoy to many countries in Southeast Asia and around the Indian Ocean. Zheng, a Muslim from Yunnan Province, had learned something about foreign countries, especially the Arab world, from his grandfather and father, who had been to Mecca as pilgrims. In 1405 he led a large

Portrait of Zheng He

fleet with 62 ships and 27,800 men, carrying gold, silk, porcelain, and other goods with them, and sailed to Java and other islands in

Southeast Asia. Then they turned west and went to India. They returned to China in 1407. After that Zheng and his fleet sailed again to these areas. Altogether they made seven voyages within 28 years (1405–1433). They went as far as the east coast of Africa, the Red Sea and Mecca. As a result, relations between China and these areas became closer and economic and cultural exchanges between them were promoted.

According to estimates, Zheng and his crew visited more than 30 countries, and he never considered the countries as "great discoveries." He colonized no country, though China was the most powerful of the world. Instead, China helped those countries with ship-building, well-sinking, manufacturing, medicine and settling their internal strife. To these countries Zheng He's voyages were friendly and peaceful.

Zheng's voyages were nearly 100 years earlier than Vasco da Gama's voyage around the Cape of Good Hope and Christopher Columbus's to the Americas, and his fleet was larger than theirs by far. This fact showed that China's technology of navigation was quite advanced at that time.

During the Ming period, along with the development of handicraft production, appeared employers who owned some equipment and craftsmen who owned nothing but labor power. The latter had to work for the former for wages. This may be regarded as the beginning of capitalism in China.

In the textile industry such relations between employers and workers were very clear. In big cities like Hangzhou, Suzhou, Nanjing and Songjiang, some small producers became rich enough to buy more looms and began to hire workers. At first these employers continued to work on their looms, but later they did no work except direct their employees. At the same time, workers who had no looms had to find jobs. If they did not have regular employers, they had to gather at a place early in the morning every day to wait for someone to hire them. In other words, there was a market for free labor power.

This capitalist mode of production also appeared in salt-making, iron-smelting, porcelain-making, ship-building, sugar-refining, and paper-making industries, and in copper and coal mines.

These seeds of capitalism failed to grow and blossom for many reasons. The most important factor that prevented their growth was the natural economy that prevailed in the whole country. Most families, especially those in the countryside, tried to be self-sufficient. They grew grain and cotton, raised pigs and chickens, wove cloth, and made most of the things they needed themselves. The old Chinese saying "Men plow and women weave" describes this simple, self-reliant life. The peasants, who

Loom, the most important tool in the textile industry, one of the Chinese industries where capitalism first emerged

made up the great majority of the population, seldom went to the market to buy things. And they were so poor that they could not afford to buy things when they wanted to. The limited market, of course, could not stimulate production.

Besides, rich landlords were not interested in industry—they usually wanted to buy land with their money. This meant that industry was short of investment. The feudal government, which represented the interests of the landlord class, did not try to encourage the development of industry or commerce; on the contrary, it often hindered their growth by imposing on them heavy taxes and various limitations. In short, capitalism could not grow in China in the Ming Dynasty because the feudal economic system and political power were too strong.

However, this new mode of production, as a new element in social life, had some influence on people's thinking, and gave people, mainly urban people, new ideas, which were reflected in certain literary works.

18

Ming Novels and Its Three Masterpieces

As has been mentioned, the Ming period saw a rapid development of handicraft industry and commerce, and this helped the growth of capitalist elements in the economy. At the same time, people, especially those in the cities, began to have new ideas, which were different from feudal traditions in one way or another. This was natural, because economic changes usually lead to changes in people's thinking.

New ideas of the period were reflected in literature. The most important literary form of the Ming was the novel written in the language spoken by the common people. The writing of fiction had begun as early as the Wei and Jin, and had flourished during the Tang. Many interesting short stories had been produced. They were all written in refined classical Chinese, which was quite different from the spoken language, and therefore difficult for ordinary readers to understand. During the Ming a great step forward was seen in fiction writing. Not only short stories, but also long novels, were written, and written in a language close to that spoken by the people.

In the Song and Yuan periods, story-telling (mixed with songs) had been very popular, especially in big cities. A crowd would gather around a story-teller and listened to his stories, which were mainly about historical events, such as those of the Three Kingdoms. As those events were very complicated, he could not finish a complete story in one sitting, and had to divide it into parts. Each part began with a topic—often a sentence or a couplet (two sentences of the same number of words and the same structure). At the end of a part, he would say, "If you want to know what happened afterward, please listen to the explanations in the next part." This form of story-telling was the origin of novels in chapters.

During the 14th century, when the Yuan was replaced by the Ming, there were writers or scholars who began to edit and polish the scripts of earlier story-tellers. The first novels in chapters were thus produced. They were *Romance of the Three Kingdoms*, *Romance of the Five Dynasties*, *Water Margin* (also translated as *Outlaws of the Marsh and All Men Are Brothers*), and a few others.

Luo Guanzhong, who wrote *Romance of the Three Kingdoms* (*Three Kingdoms* for short), was born in Taiyuan, Shanxi. The dates of his birth and death are uncertain; probably he lived between 1310 and 1385. It was said that he once worked for Zhang Shicheng, one of the leaders of the peasant uprisings toward the end of the Yuan. After Zhang failed, he devoted himself to writing historical novels.

He disliked the stories about the Three Kingdoms told by professional story-tellers, because their language was too crude

"Three Heroes Combating Lv Bu" in *Romance of the Three Kingdoms*

and they were often not true to history. He decided to write a novel about this period of history based on reliable historical works in a language that was neither too difficult for ordinary readers nor too crude for well-educated people. The book he wrote was the first historical novel in Chinese written by a scholar, and the first novel written for the ordinary people. For this we can say that he was a writer with a progressive point of view. The book was later further revised and polished by other writers.

It would be impossible to find out how many different editions, let alone how many copies, of the book have been printed, or how many operas based on it have been produced, over the past 600 years. The book has been so popular that almost everyone who can read has read it. Even children know something about its main heroes as a result of seeing operas or listening to stories about the Three Kingdoms.

Luo Guanzhong praises Liu Bei and his generals and advisers, and criticises Cao Cao. Before Luo there had been different views on these historical figures. It seems that Luo considers Liu the rightful ruler of the country, not only because he was a descendant of the Han rulers, but also because he was kind-hearted, sincere and loved the people, while Cao was tricky, cunning, and despotic, according to his descriptions. Perhaps Luo intended to show the people's love and support for good rulers and their hatred of evil ones. Whether Liu was so good and Cao was so bad in real life as they are described in the book is of course another question.

The book gives detailed descriptions of many tricks and intrigues, the plotting and scheming of the rulers or leaders of the period. Such descriptions could be useful to those who wanted to use tricks in achieving their aims; at the same time, they helped ordinary readers to see what their rulers or oppressors were really like.

Real heroes, of whom Zhuge Liang and Guan Yu are representative, are described as people who are loyal and brave, active and resourceful in political and military struggles. They were taken as examples in later ages by many officials and military men who were devoted to their causes.

Important characters in the book are impressive and unforgettable. They become alive when they act and talk. In other words, the writer succeeds in describing them with their own behavior. Readers seem to understand their thoughts and motives though there is very little description of their mental states.

According to a Qing historian, the whole book is made up of 70 percent of history and 30 percent of fiction. The combination of truth and imagination is common to most historical novels.

At about the same time when *Three Kingdoms* was written, there appeared another historical novel: *Water Margin*.

Heroes of Liangshan in *Water Margin*

The revolt of Song Jiang and his followers was a historical fact. There are brief records of it in various histories of the Song Dynasty. Later it became a popular topic of story-tellers. Toward the end of the Yuan, there were peasant revolts in many parts of the country, and people liked to talk about heroes and events in those revolts. Perhaps this situation made Shi Nai'an think of writing a novel about Song Jiang's revolt.

About Shi's life there has been no record at all. He is believed to have lived in the 14th century and taken part in a peasant uprising. He put together the disconnected stories and episodes about Song Jiang and his friends told in scripts for story-tellers, reorganized them, and wove out of them a connected and complete novel.

The novel exposes the corruption and crimes of members of the ruling class and makes it clear that their power and wealth were built on the sufferings of the oppressed people. They often made it impossible for good and honest people to live a decent life, and forced them to go to Liangshan and become outlaws. Lin Chong's story is a good example.

Many other heroes, like Wu Song, Li Kui and Lu Zhishen, are also forced by corrupt officials or evil landlords to go to Liangshan to join Song Jiang. Most of them come from very poor families. Although they are called "bandits" by the government, they are in fact honorable people with a strong sense of justice and great courage, ready to help the poor and weak to fight against their oppressors.

The book describes the entire process of a peasant uprising: its beginning, growth, and end. It helps readers to understand the feudal system and feudal society. They are able to learn from it what they cannot learn from ordinary historical works. For it describes people of all classes, from high-ranking government officials to poor peasants, and their relations and conflicts, in a very concrete and striking way.

The language of the book is the language spoken by the people, more colloquial than that of *Three Kingdoms*. In the latter literary classical Chinese is often used, because that is the language of the upper-class people portrayed in it. The description of characters in *Water Margin* may be more successful than that in *Three Kingdoms*. Most of the heroes are ordinary men and women who grow into resolute fighters on the side of the poor people. They change, awaken and mature as a result of the oppression they have borne and the struggle they have waged. Their growth is real and convincing. No wonder the book has been as popular as *Three Kingdoms* ever since it was written.

Two centuries later, a novel of a different type appeared. It was written by Wu Cheng'en, who lived between 1500 and 1583. He was born in Huai'an, Jiangsu Province. In his childhood and youth, he was deeply interested in myths and strange stories about gods and monsters. About this special interest he wrote, "I have liked to read strange and amazing stories ever since I was a child. For fear of my father and teacher scolding me and taking the books away from me, I used to hide myself in some out-of-the-way place to read them. When I was grown up, my brain was filled almost entirely with strange and amazing tales." Then he wrote that when he was writing strange tales, he was quite amused. "It seems that strange tales have asked to be written, instead of my seeking to write them."

His great work was *Journey to the West*. It is a novel about the famous Tang monk Xuanzang going to India to study and collect Buddhist texts. There had been many tales and legends about the monk's trip before Wu's time, and Wu drew on them. But he recreated the whole story, changing it from a religious story to a mythological or legendary tale, which to a certain extent reflects the society of his time.

The hero of the novel is of course Sun Wukong, or Monkey King. He is full of rebellion, having no respect or fear for authorities. Gods and Buddhas try to maintain their law and order, but Monkey King does not obey them; he despises them. On his way to the west, he fights and defeats all kinds of evil spirits and monsters. He

Sun Wukong in *Journey to the West*

never bows before enemies that look terrible or difficulties that seem too great to overcome. This stubborn fighting spirit is passionately described and praised in the book. Perhaps the author wishes to see the same spirit in the people oppressed by men just as evil as the monsters Monkey King has to face and fight.

In telling the story, Wu uses the language of the street and market place, and it is very lively and vivid.

The publication of these three novels—*Romance of the Three Kingdoms*, *Water Margin*, and *Journey to the West*—was a great event in Ming culture. It marked the beginning of a new stage in the history of Chinese literature.

19

The Rise of Southern Drama and Great Advance of Short Fictions in the Ming Dynasty

During the Yuan period, while *zaju* or northern drama was developing in the north, a different type of drama was taking shape and spreading in the south with Wenzhou, Zhejiang, as its center. Southern drama, as it was called, had its beginnings in the Northern Song. Using southern dialects and southern folk songs, it was popular among the ordinary people of Zhejiang and its neighboring provinces, including Fujian, Jiangsu and Anhui. Only a few complete works of southern drama have been preserved, partly because literary men of the Song and Yuan looked down upon this form of drama and would not try to write plays for it, and partly because northern drama was the main trend and attracted greater attention.

If those few southern plays are compared with northern plays, some of the differences between these two types of drama can be seen. In a northern play, there are usually four acts, and only one actor or actress sings in one act, and the other actors and actresses talk but do not sing. Besides, one rhyme is used in all the songs in one act. In a southern play, the number of scenes is flexible: there may be only a few and there may also be as many as forty or fifty scenes. In one scene more than one actor or actress may sing, and sometimes two or more of them may sing together, and the songs in one scene may have different rhymes. In short, there is greater freedom in arrangement and form in southern drama.

Toward the end of the Yuan and at the beginning of the Ming there appeared some good southern plays, of which the best known is the *Story of the Pipa* by Gao Ming. It tells the story of how the filial and faithful Zhao Wuniang goes alone to the capital with a *pipa* to find her husband Cai Bojie, who has passed the imperial examinations, has become a government official, and

Portrait of Tang Xianzu

married the prime minister's daughter.

During the Ming, northern drama was on the decline and southern drama flourished. Many important writers took an interest in southern drama and wrote plays. The most outstanding among them was Tang Xianzu (1550–1616).

Tang was born in Linchuan, Jiangxi. Having passed the imperial examinations, he got only position of a low rank, because he hated to please powerful people. Finally he had to retire and went back to his hometown, to devote himself to writing. He wrote four plays, which are all connected with dreams, so collectively they are called the "Four Dreams of Linchuan."

The Peony Pavilion, one of the "Four Dreams of Linchuan," is his masterpiece. Du Liniang, the heroine, is the daughter of a high-ranking official. In her father's big house she lives a very dull and unhappy life. The feudal ethical code and the strict rules laid down by her father deprive her of all freedom. One spring day, urged by her maid, she goes to her family garden for a walk. There she is delighted and also surprised by the beauty of nature. As she is tired, she dozes off and has a dream. In it she meets a young scholar named Liu Mengmei, and falls in love with him. When she wakes up, she knows clearly that the dream will never come true. After that she falls ill with a sad heart, and finally she dies. Three years later, the young scholar she dreamed of comes to her city on his way to the capital to take the imperial examinations. He happens to pick up the portrait Liniang painted of herself, and at night he meets Liniang's ghost. She tells him that he should open her grave at once. So he does, and Liniang comes out of the grave, a living lady as beautiful as she ever was. They are then married and begin their happy life together.

A still of the Peking opera *the Peony Pavilion*

The plot seems unreal, but it reveals a very bold new spirit: a young woman from an upper-class family dares to love a young man in spite of all traditions. She not only loves the young man, but dies for him and becomes alive again for him. She is really a woman with new ideas, and Tang Xianzu in portraying such a splendid heroine shows himself to be a dramatist who defies old beliefs.

We have talked about two important periods in the development of fiction: the Tang Dynasty, when short stories were written in refined classical Chinese, and the early and middle Ming Dynasty when long novels like *Three Kingdoms* appeared. There was another important development in the Ming in the field of fiction: the writing of short stories in plain spoken Chinese.

In the Song and Yuan, short stories had been told and sung by story-tellers to crowds gathered around them. There were story-tellers' notes; as they were not written by experienced writers, their language is generally rather crude. During the Ming, certain writers began to polish those notes and write new stories. In the last years of the Ming Dynasty there was a great advance in short fiction.

During this period the man who made the greatest contribution to the growth of short fiction was Feng Menglong (1574–1646). He was born in Suzhou, Jiangsu. For some time he was a county magistrate, but all his life he was a passionate lover of literature, especially fiction. He collected, edited, revised and published a great number of short stories, plays and folk tales. The first collection of short stories he edited was originally called *Ancient and Modern Stories*. When the second and third collections came out, he entitled them *Ordinary Words to Warn the World* and *Lasting Words to Awaken the World*. Then he

Three Volumes of Words

changed the title of the first collection to *Clear Words to Illustrate the World*. The three volumes were then given a general title: *Three Volumes of Words*.

In these three volumes are collected 120 short stories based on earlier story-tellers' notes and revised or rewritten by Feng. As a result of his work, those stories are not only interesting but also readable. Most of them reflect life in prosperous cities, and most of the characters are people of the lower and middle classes. Some of the stories describe young people who are faithful to those they love; some describe craftsmen, vendors and small merchants who are willing to make sacrifices to help their friends; others expose the crimes of corrupt officials and big landlords, and the conflicts within feudal families. They are like mirrors in which the reader can see what urban life was like, and how people of different classes lived and behaved in the Ming and earlier periods.

Take the story of the oil vendor Qin Zhong, for example. He is poor and very low on the social ladder, but he wins the love of a beautiful prostitute Shen Yaoqin, because he is sincere and loves her wholeheartedly. When Shen compares this poor young man with those sons of wealthy families who treat her as a plaything and insult her, she sees the meaning and value of true love, and decides to marry Qin. This story shows a change in urban people's attitude toward marriage: sincere love is more important than wealth and social position, and in this theme lies the significance of the story.

When Feng Menglong was editing his stories, another writer was doing similar work. Ling Mengchu (1580–1644) was born in Huzhou, Zhejiang. Like Feng, he was a lover and promoter of popular literature. He compiled two volumes of short stories called *Surprising Stories to Make One Slap the Desk*, or *Two Volumes of Slapping* for short. He wrote most of the 78 stories in them, though the material came from earlier folk tales.

Later, a man who called himself the Old Man Hugging the Jar selected 40 from the nearly 200 stories in the "Three Volumes of Words" and "Two Volumes of Slapping" and put them together in

"Three Volumes of Words and Two Volumes of Slapping"

a book entitled *Wonderful Sights, Ancient and Modern*, which was to become more popular than the five original books.

20

Ming and Early Qing Thinkers: the Yangming School and Outstanding Progressive Scholars

One of the best-known Ming philosophers was Wang Shouren (1472–1529), and Yangming was his courtesy name. He was born in Yuyao, Zhejiang. In his youth he studied Zhu Xi's works and was greatly inspired by them. Later he became a government official. More than once, he took military action against revolting peasants in Jiangxi and Guangxi, and after much fighting he suppressed them. About

Portrait of Wang Shouren

this experience he said, "It is easy to wipe out the 'bandits' in the mountains, but difficult to wipe out the bandits in the mind." Obviously he meant that thought control should be strengthened.

While serving in the government, he taught students. He discussed with them questions of philosophy, especially the theories of principle, which had been the main trend of philosophy ever since the Northern Song. His students made records of his sayings and published them, and he also wrote a few books himself.

He started the Yangming school of philosophy. Essentially his theory is a development of Lu Jiuyuan's theory of the mind. He agreed with Lu that the mind is principle. "There is no object outside the mind," he said, "and there is no principle outside the mind." He asked, "Who would know the sky is high or the earth is low if there was no mind?"

Another important theory Wang advanced is that of innate knowledge. According to him, every man is born with the knowledge of what is truth and what is virtue, and every man has the innate ability to distinguish between good and evil, right and wrong. Sages do not have more of this innate knowledge than ordinary people, so everyone could be a sage. In this way he broke down the barrier between sages and ordinary people, and encouraged later thinkers to adopt new ideas.

His third important theory is the unity of knowledge and action. Philosophers before him, like Zhu Xi and Lu Jiuyuan, had held that knowledge came before action, but Wang said that knowledge and action are the two sides of the same thing: there is action within knowledge and knowledge within action. He said that knowledge is the beginning of action and action the completion of knowledge. They are inseparable. In short, Wang had his own view on the relationship between knowledge and action or practice. Today it is generally believed that knowledge comes from practice and practice tests the correctness of knowledge.

After Emperor Chengzu (Zhu Di) most of the Ming emperors were poor rulers. Many of them were corrupt or ignorant. Emperor Shenzong, for instance, ordered tens of thousands of workers and peasants to build a large underground palace to be used as his grave. This project cost so much money that it would have been enough to feed ten million people for a year. The last Ming emperors were too busy with their luxurious and immoral life to take care of state affairs. The government was often under the control of evil eunuchs, who oppressed and persecuted officials and people opposed to them.

Then, what had happened toward the end of many dynasties happened again: There was famine in some areas, but tax collectors forced the people to pay rent and taxes, and the people took up arms to protect themselves. In 1627 peasant revolts broke out in northern Shaanxi. Soon they spread to Shanxi and Henan. In 1635 the leaders of many peasant armies held a meeting in Xingyang, Henan, to plan their strategies. This was the first joint meeting of peasant armies in Chinese history.

Li Zicheng, the most outstanding leader of the peasant armies, occupied Xi'an and the whole of Shaanxi Province in 1644. There he declared the founding of a state called Dashun. Then he moved east into Shanxi and Hebei, and finally his army entered Beijing. The last Ming emperor hanged himself on the hill north of the imperial palace. That was the end of the Ming Dynasty.

Li stayed in Beijing only for only about 40 days. He and his men failed to work out a policy to deal with the complicated situation they were facing. In the Northeast the Manchus were making preparations for an invasion. Remnant Ming forces were still fighting the peasant armies in many places, and a small Ming court had been set up in Nanjing. To make matters worse, some of his generals and advisers began to live and behave like corrupt officials; they even seized money and women.

Wu Sangui, the Ming general guarding the Shanhaiguan Pass, surrendered to the Manchus, and led them into the Great Wall to attack the peasant army. Li Zicheng had to leave Beijing and go west to Shanxi. He was pursued by the Manchu troops and the Ming armies that had joined the Manchu forces. Finally he was killed in Hubei when he was only 39 years old.

The Manchus, whose ancestors, the Nüzhen ethnic group, had founded the Jin in the Song period, had lived in the Northeast for centuries. In 1616 they were unified under Nurhachi, and in 1636 Huangtaiji, his son, established a state called Qing. Militarily the Qing grew stronger and stronger and was the main threat to the security of the Ming Dynasty. After its troops entered the Great Wall with the help of Wu Sangui and occupied Beijing, the Qing moved its capital there from Shenyang. Many Ming officials and officers would rather cooperate with the Qing in fighting the peasant armies than help the peasant armies to resist the Qing. In a few years' time nearly the whole country was brought under Qing's control. The small Ming court in Nanjing, disunited and corrupt, had been crushed by Qing forces in 1644.

The last area taken over by the Qing was Taiwan. In 1661 Zheng Chenggong, a Ming general, sailed across the strait to Taiwan and drove away the Dutch colonialists, who had occupied the island for about 40 years. Zheng carried out political, economic and cultural reconstruction in Taiwan, intending to make it a base for fighting the Qing. His work promoted the economic development of the island, but he was not able to return to the mainland before he died in 1662. His son and then his grandson continued his work.

Portrait of Zheng Chenggong

In the 16th century, European traders began to cast their greedy eyes on East Asia. Among the earliest arrivals were those from Portugal and Spain, followed by Dutch and English merchants. Their commercial activities were accompanied by piratical crimes; they attacked, plundered and occupied some East Asian countries. In 1553 Portuguese merchants, by deceiving and bribing some Ming officials, got the right to stay in Macao. The number of Portuguese there quickly increased to over ten thousand. Thus began the Portuguese occupation of this port.

At the same time, European missionaries also came. In 1580 a group of Jesuits, or members of the Society of Jesus, an organization within the Roman Catholic Church, came to China to do missionary work. Later more Jesuits came. As a result of their work, a number of Chinese became Catholics (totaling 150,000 in 1650). But missionary activities were banned by the early Qing emperors.

The best-known of the Jesuits was an Italian called Matteo Ricci (1552–1610). He first worked in Zhaoqing, Guangdong; then he came to Beijing, where he was allowed to set up a church by a Ming emperor. He had contact with some Ming scholars and officials. The books he had brought with him on mathematics, surveying, water conservancy, etc, were translated by

Portrait of Matteo Ricci

those Chinese scholars close to him. This had some positive influence on the development of science of the time.

In the middle of the 17th century, when the Ming was replaced by the Qing, there appeared a new trend of thought among the scholars. Two factors made this possible. One was the fall of the Ming, which made many scholars sad. They wanted to find out the causes of and draw lessons from this tragic event. The other was the seeds of capitalism that had emerged during the Ming and the new ideas that had come with this social change. As has been mentioned, Ming drama and fiction show the influence of this change, and naturally, it was to be reflected in the thinking of philosophers.

Some of the thinkers of the early Qing period began to see

the weaknesses of traditional ideas, especially those of the school of principle, which had dominated Chinese thought ever since the Northern Song. Some of them even realized that there was something wrong with feudal rule and Confucianism. Later historians compared this new trend of thought to the Enlightenment Movement in Europe in the 18th century. That movement brought to Europe new ideas of democracy and science and helped to push many European countries forward along the road of modernization.

Outstanding among the progressive scholars of the time were Huang Zongxi, Gu Yanwu and Wang Fuzhi.

Huang Zongxi (1610–1695), born in Yuyao, Zhejiang, was the son of a high-ranking Ming official who was killed by an evil head of the eunuchs. After the fall of Beijing to Manchu troops, Huang Zongxi joined those who resisted the invaders. They failed to save the Ming, and Huang decided to be an independent scholar and teacher. He refused all offers of employment from the Qing rulers.

Portrait of Huang Zongxi

Huang studied and had profound knowledge of the classics, history, literature, astronomy, mathematics and music. He wrote several important works on philosophy and history.

About the relationship between *qi* (material force) and *li* (principle), he said that the universe is nothing but *qi*, and that there would be no *li* without *qi*. He said that *li* is the principle of material force, and it is not an independent substance. In this way he refuted the wrong view held by the school of principle: there was *li* before *qi*, or before the universe came into being.

His criticism of feudal rule and the imperial institutions show him to be a brave thinker. He said that the emperor and his ministers should work for the well-being of the people, not for the satisfaction of the desires of the emperor. The emperor, he said, was not the master of his ministers, who should not be blindly obedient to him. Laws should be made for the benefit of the country. But many laws had been made to strengthen the rule by one family. The result was that the more laws there were, the greater the confusion. Such laws in fact led to lawlessness. He held that the powers of the prime minister should be increased so as to limit the powers of the emperor, and that schools should be turned into organs where government decisions could be discussed. "What the emperor considers right may not be right, and what the emperor considers wrong may not be wrong." he said.

Obviously he saw the evils of the feudal political system, under which the whole country and all the people were treated like the emperor's private property. He called for reform. In his ideas there was a clear democratic element.

He pointed out that the taxes imposed on the people were too heavy. They had to be reduced to make it easier for the people to earn a living. He said that both industry and commerce were foundations of the economy, just like agriculture. The economic policy of all dynasties had taken agriculture as the foundation and industry and commerce as unimportant additions. Huang's view clearly reflected the sentiments of the merchants and employers of craftsmen of his day.

Gu Yanwu (1613–1682) was born in Kunshan, Jiangsu. Like

Huang Zongxi, he joined the forces that resisted the invading Manchu troops. It was said that his foster-mother starved herself to death rather than live under Manchu rule. On her deathbed she told Yanwu not to serve the Qing Dynasty as an official. Yanwu remained true to her wishes. He spent the rest of his

Portrait of Gu Yanwu

life trying to organize anti-Qing activities and writing books. One of his best-known works is *Record of Daily Knowledge*.

Gu criticized the philosophy of principle, which, he said, was just like Zen Buddhism. Scholars of that school were interested in empty talk about human nature and the mind, and would not study real problems or ways of self-cultivation. They had very harmful influence on people's thinking. Based on his own experience in political struggle, Gu took two maxims from *The Analects* and considered them the guide for all people. They were "one should study extensively" and "one should have a sense of shame in conduct." According to his explanation, one should study what is useful, from the right ways of behavior to the ways of educating people and governing the country, and one should write things that help to change customs and achieve ideal government. About the sense of shame, he said it meant a sense of responsibility for the prosperity and decline of one's country, and this sense should guide everything one does and one's relations with all other people. In other words, one should adhere to lofty principles and should never do anything unjust or shameful. It is clear that his intention was to awaken people to the shame of remaining passive under Qing rule.

Gu also expressed his views on certain philosophical problems. He said that *qi* fills the universe, and that *dao* or the Way exists only in concrete objects.

Wang Fuzhi (1619–1692) was born in Hengyang, Hunan. When the Manchu troops came south, he organized resistance in southern Hunan. After he failed, he lived in hiding in the mountains of western Hunan. Then he returned to Hengyang and devoted his time to writing. Altogether he wrote more than a hundred books, dealing with philosophy, history, religion and the classics.

His greatest contribution is in the field of philosophy. His thought embodies the spirit of his time and

Portrait of Wang Fuzhi

represents the highest achievement in philosophical studies of the 17th century.

In criticizing the school of principle, he said that principle is nothing but the principle of material force. There is no principle outside or independent of material force, and there is no principle of a thing before the thing comes into being. It was impossible for there to be the principle of archery before there were bows and arrows. Similarly, it was impossible for there to be the principle of the father before there was a son. In short, there is no principle without an instrument. Principles are derived from concrete objects or social reality. These views are entirely different from those of the school of principle, and are comparable to those held by the materialist school in modern times.

He further pointed out that motion is absolute while the static state is relative. The static state contains motion, but motion does not contain the static state. The water in rivers seems static, but the water in them today is not the water in them in the past. Man's skin, hair, and muscles are changing all the time, though it can hardly be noticed.

This view of change also applies to social life. "The Han and Tang dynasties did not have the customs of today," he said, "similarly, people today do not have many of the customs of future years." Wu, Chu, Min and Yue had been areas inhabited by backward ethnic groups in ancient times, but they were centers of culture and education. Therefore both natural and social histories show that everything changes. What makes things change or move is the opposite forces within them, like *yin* and *yang*, the hard and the soft, the cold and the warm, what gives birth and what kills.

His theory of change and development was advanced and progressive not only in China, but also in the whole world in the 17th century.

About human nature, he also had views different from those of Song philosophers like Zhu Xi, who held that human desire was opposite to "heavenly principle," and man had to get rid of human desire to adhere to the latter. Wang said that human desire and heavenly principle are not really different. "Sages have desire, which is also heavenly principle," he said. "Heaven has no desire, and its principle is also human desire."

As he lived and wrote his books in a remote village, none of his works were published in his lifetime. After his death, his son managed to get some of them printed. It was after the Opium War that his complete works were published and widely circulated. Many patriotic scholars of the 19th century turned to him for guidance and inspiration. His influence was then clearly felt. He should be regarded as the leading Chinese philosopher of the 17th century.

21

Early Qing Fiction and Drama

During the reign of Shunzhi and Kangxi (1644–1722), the Qing rulers tried hard to unify and stabilize the country. They adopted a series of military and political measures to strengthen their rule, and to a large extent they succeeded. The central and local governments were reorganized; laws were made and administered; officials of all levels were appointed. Although people of all ethnic groups were chosen as officials, the Manchu aristocrats formed the core of the regime.

To unify people's thought, the early Qing rulers, including Kangxi, Yongzheng and Qianlong, continued the Chinese tradition of honoring Confucius and Confucianism. Confucian scholars, especially those who believed in and spread the philosophy of principle, were praised and respected. They could pass the imperial examinations, which had been restored to recruit officials from among scholars. At the same time, the Qing rulers banned books which they thought were harmful to their rule, and punished and even killed a number of scholars who were considered disloyal or opposed to them.

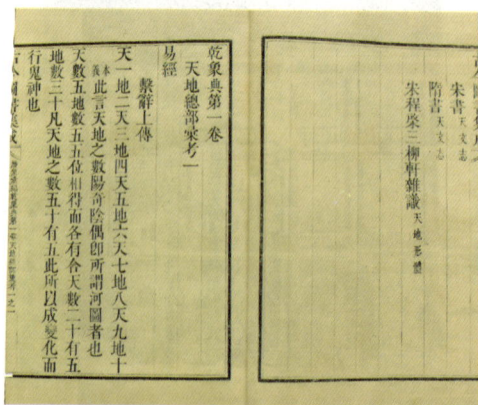

A Collection of Books of Ancient and Modern Times

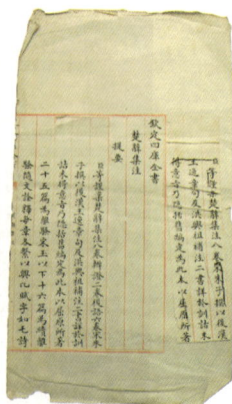

Complete Library of the Four Treasuries

During the reign of Yongzheng and Qianlong (1722–1795), the Qing government started two huge cultural projects: the compilation of *A Collection of Books of Ancient and Modern Times* and the editing of the *Complete Library of the Four Treasuries*. The former, completed in 1725, consisted of 10,000 volumes divided into six major parts and 6,109 items according to content. The latter, completed in 1782, ten years after the work began, consisted of 79,337 volumes, divided into four major parts (or treasuries): Confucian classics, histories, philosophical works and literary works. This great project helped to preserve many valuable books, but those disliked by the Qing rulers were not included.

In spite of the thought control imposed by the government, men of letters produced many excellent works, especially stories and plays, in the first hundred years of the Qing Dynasty. The literary traditions of the Ming were valued and carried on by Qing writers. Besides, some of them had desired to express their dissatisfaction at and hatred of Manchu rule. So their works not only had high literary merit, but also contained progressive views.

One such writer was Pu Songling (1640–1715), who wrote *Strange Tales from a Scholar's Studio*. Born into a declining landlord family in Zibo, Shandong, Pu lived a hard life almost all his life. He had to work as a secretary for an official or teach students at a landlord's house far from home with low pay. Even after he was 60 years old, he still had to walk long distances to places where there was work to do.

Talented as he was, he could not pass the imperial examinations or find a government post. As a result, he lived among the ordinary people most of the time and understood their life and feelings, their likes and dislikes. This helped him to write many of the stories collected in *Strange Tales from a Scholar's Studio*.

In the book there are over 400 stories. Many of them are about ghosts and foxes, but in telling them

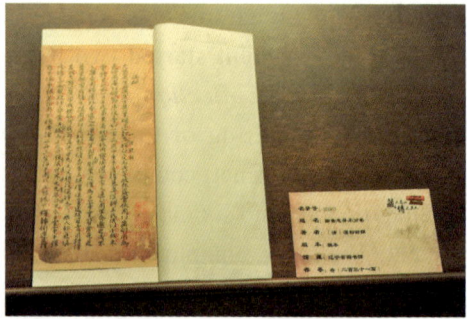

Strange Tales from a Scholar's Studio

the writer's real intention is to expose the darkness of human society, the corruption of officials, and the hypocrisy and injustice of the imperial examination system. There are also stories about young people longing for true love but prevented from getting it by feudal customs and traditions.

"The Cricket," one of the stories, tells how an emperor, who liked cricket fighting, forced local officials to present strong crickets to him and how the people suffered because of this hobby of the emperor's. An honest man by the name of Cheng Ming could not find a good cricket and the local official ordered him to buy one. For this Cheng was almost broke. Then he luckily found a strong cricket, but his careless young son killed it. Severely scolded by his father, the son wanted to commit suicide. He was saved, and lay in bed unconscious for a long time. Then Cheng Ming found a cricket good at fighting, which he presented to the emperor through various officials. This changed the fate of Cheng Ming's family. Finally his son regained consciousness and told his parents that he had turned into a cricket and had fought and defeated many other crickets in the imperial palace.

What a terrible picture this story draws of feudal rule! To

satisfy a small desire of the ruler, innocent people had to face ruin and death. This shows the depth and sharpness of the writer's criticism of the unjust society.

Pu Songling wrote all his stories in beautiful and vivid classical Chinese. He departed from the practice of telling stories in the spoken language started by the Ming novelists and story-tellers, but continued the tradition of Tang writers of short fiction. After him some other writers wrote stories in the classical style, but their works were hardly comparable with his strange tales.

In Pu's time there were two well-known dramatists producing excellent plays. They were Hong Sheng (1645–1704) and Kong Shangren (1648–1718). Hong was born in Hangzhou, Zhejiang, lived in Beijing for a long time without any success in his political career, and became famous when he was over 40 years old because of his play *Palace of Eternal Life*. Then he did something that happened to make the emperor angry, and he had to leave the capital and return to Hangzhou to spend his last years.

Palace of Eternal Life mainly describes the love between Emperor Xuanzong (Minghuang) of the Tang and his concubine Yang Yuhuan. After Yang's death, the emperor missed her day and night. Finally both of them, on orders from the Jade Emperor, rose to Heaven and became an eternal couple there. The play also describes the corruption and conflict of the ruling class and its oppression of the people. So besides the love theme the play has a political theme, which is valuable in a way. But these two themes, according to some critics, do not strengthen, but weaken each other.

Kong Shangren was born in Qufu, Shandong, a distant descendant of Confucius. He worked for some time in the Central University in Beijing, and later he was sent to the Yangtze River

A still of the Kunqu opera *Palace of Eternal Life*

valley to help with flood control. While visiting Nanjing and Yangzhou, he learned much about the fall of the Southern Ming, and began to think of writing a play about it. After he returned to Beijing, he devoted his time to writing the play *The Peach Blossom Fan*. It was a great success. Perhaps because of this he was dismissed from his post. He then returned to Qufu to live a quiet life as a common citizen.

The Peach Blossom Fan is a historical romance, based on the events of the short-lived Southern Ming regime in Nanjing. When Beijing had fallen to the Manchu army, some Ming ministers and generals helped a Ming prince ascend the throne in Nanjing. This was the beginning of the Southern Ming. While the Manchu army was marching south, important men in the Nanjing regime were not trying to organize resistance. On the contrary, they were becoming more and more corrupt, seizing wealth and power, seeking pleasure and paying no attention to the critical situation facing them. Within a year this regime collapsed.

The play gives a faithful account of this tragedy. Woven into the historical events is the love affair between Li Xiangjun, a beautiful and talented prostitute, and Hou Fangyu, a well-known scholar of the time. Faithful to the man she loved, Li was determined not to marry anyone else. She hated those evil men in the Nanjing government. Once one of them tried to force her to be his concubine. She resolutely refused, and knocked her head against the floor, intending to kill herself. Her blood splashed over a fan given her by Hou. She did not die; nor did she go to that official's home. A friend of hers, who was a painter, drew branches on the fan and turned her blood drops into peach flowers—a painting that was a symbol of her devotion and resolution.

A still of the Kunqu opera *The Peach Blossom Fan*

It is clear that by writing the play Kong Shangren intended to reveal the real causes of the fall of the Southern Ming, so as to help people to draw lessons from it. The play shows his patriotic sentiments and deep understanding of the history and social change of this period.

About half a century after Hong and Kong wrote their plays, the popular satirical novel *The Scholars* was written by Wu Jingzi (1701–1754). Wu was born in Quanjiao, Anhui. His father was an honest scholar, uninterested in fame and wealth. After his father's death, he became poor and had to sell what property he had inherited. Then he moved to Nanjing, and lived a poor life there. He would not take the imperial examinations simply because he looked down upon them. In Nanjing and Yangzhou, which he often visited, he got to know many officials and scholars who had passed the examinations, and learned that many of these people were shamefully selfish, and would not hesitate to use underhand methods for their own interests. They provided him with material for the novel he was going to write. In his last years he studied Confucian classics and wrote something about them, but what he wrote was lost after he died.

A learned scholar himself, Wu saw through the attractive masks put on by those scholars who were shallow and hypocritical. In the novel he describes many "scholars" who did everything they could to pass the imperial examinations first and then climb the social ladder and make money. As they had neither learning nor moral integrity, they could only serve the ruling class as lackeys.

Fan Jin, one of the characters, had sat for the imperial examinations more than 20 times without success. He was looked down upon by all his relatives and neighbors. Then one day news came that he had passed. He was so excited that he was out of his senses. To sober him up, his father-in-law, a butcher, slapped him on the face. After this farce, he quickly became important and rich, and squeezed into the official circle to oppress the common people.

Wu wrote the book at a time when the Qing rulers had consolidated their power, and were trying to buy over scholars by giving them government posts through the imperial examinations. Wu hated this system and had only contempt for those who wanted to benefit from it.

"Fan Jin Passed the Imperial Examinations" in *The Scholars*

The novel may be called a work of critical realism. Its main objective is to show the dark side of society and expose evil people, while earlier novels, like *Three Kingdoms* and *Water Margin*, mainly describe heroes who embody good moral qualities. *The Scholars* marked the beginning of satirical fiction in China's literary history.

22

Cao Xueqin and Dream of the Red Mansions

Cao Xueqin Memorial Hall, Beijing

Cao Xueqin (1715–1763), who wrote *Dream of the Red Mansions*, was born into the family of a very rich and important official-chief commissioner of the Nanjing Silk Bureau. This enviable post was given by the Qing rulers first to his great grandfather, and then to his grandfather and father. During his six inspection tours to the South, Emperor Kangxi stayed in their residence four times, which showed Cao Xueqin their close relations with the emperor and the luxury of their family. Brought up in such a family, Xueqin led the life of the most privileged people in his childhood. When he grew up, however, his fate drastically changed. His father fell out of the favor of the rulers, was dismissed from his post, and quickly became unimportant and poor. Xueqin moved from Nanjing to Beijing, and lived in a small house in the western suburb of the city, "eating porridge and drinking wine bought on credit," as he said of his own life. It was during this time that he began to write his immortal novel. Unfortunately, before he could finish it, he died of illness in poverty. He wrote the first 80 chapters. Later, almost 30 years after his death, a scholar-official called Gao E added 40 chapters to Cao's work, and made the story complete. Thus the edition of 120 chapters came into being.

Cao's experience in his childhood made him familiar with the lifestyle and customs of the aristocrat. The decline of his

Lin Daiyu in *Dream of the Red Mansions*

family and adverse conditions of his later years helped him to see the corruption and decadence of the people in his early memories. With this experience and understanding he was able to paint a most broad, varied, truthful and colorful picture of the society of his day.

In the novel there are all kinds of characters: hypocritical but self-righteous aristocrats, their arrogant and prodigal sons, their commanding and lazy wives and daughters, their humble and obedient servants and maids, flattering officials and scholars, poor peasants who have to hand over large parts of their harvests to their lords, merchants and actors, monks and nuns. In short, the novel shows a cross section of the urban and rural communities of Cao's time.

Of all the people in the Jia house, Baoyu and Daiyu are most carefully described. Their love for each other and dislike of the social environment form the main thread that runs through the whole novel.

What is special about Baoyu is that he hates the traditions and moral codes of his family. He refuses to take the road of life that his family has chosen for him. In a sense he is a rebel of his class. "Women's bones and flesh are made of water," he says, "and men's bones and flesh are made of mud. Women give me the impression of cleanness, but men stink offensively." This shows that he is disgusted with those men who are after fame and wealth, and sees innocence and purity in women.

Daiyu is a sensitive and sentimental girl. She shares many of Baoyu's views on life and society. She loves him, but this love is frowned upon and opposed by the older generation in control of the family, thus bringing her endless sorrows and sufferings, and finally causing her early death. Her tragedy reveals the cruelty of feudal prejudices and practices.

Besides Baoyu and Daiyu, Baochai is also a main character in the novel. She upholds all the moral principles of feudal society, and this wins her the favor of those who decide the family affairs, including Baoyu's grandmother and parents. Arranged by them, she is married to Baoyu, but the marriage does not bring her any happiness. After Baoyu leaves the family, she lives a sad, lonely life, and is made another victim of the feudal system.

Xue Baochai in *Dream of the Red Mansions*

Those lords and ladies like Jia She and Wang Xifeng try hard to defend the feudal traditions and make themselves look respectable and virtuous, but they are capable of doing all kinds of evil things. Xifeng, for instance, commits a great wrong to a loving couple, separates them and causes their death, in return for a bribery of a large amount of money. Many men in the family, old and young, lead a shamefully

Wang Xifeng in *Dream of the Red Mansions*

immoral life. So one of the old servants in the house says, "In the whole Jia house only the two stone lions are clean."

Their luxurious life is made possible by their ruthless exploitation of peasants and other working people. In one chapter it is described how the peasants working on their land are forced to give them grain, animals, money, and many other things as rent. One of the men in the Jia family even said to them, "These years we have lost much money. You have to make up the deficit for us. Who else can we ask?"

The writer shows deep sympathy for the victims of feudal oppression, especially women like Daiyu and maids like Qingwen and Yuanyang. At the same time, he mercilessly exposes the true nature of the oppressors and exploiters. All the events described in the novel point to the fact that feudalism, which had lasted for 2,000 years, was becoming rotten, and was about to start going downhill. The Jia family is a mirror that reflects this historical process.

The novel is written in beautiful colloquial Chinese based on the dialect of Beijing, spattered with dialogues and poems in classical Chinese to reflect the literary achievements of some of the characters. The plot of the novel, which consists of hundreds of incidents in daily life, is so

Qingwen in *Dream of the Red Mansions*

well woven that there seems to be no break in the continuous development of the story. In these incidents, trivial or important, the personalities of the characters are clearly shown. All the conversations between the characters help to make them real individuals who are different from one another. As one reads on, one seems to understand each character better and better, and has the impression that anything said or done by a character is what he or she ought to say or do on that special occasion. To many readers the novel is so meaningful and interesting that they cannot help reading it again and again.

The content and meaning of the novel are so rich and profound, and it has aroused so much interest among scholars that a special kind of learning generally called "Red Studies" started shortly after the novel was published, and has been continued to this day. Various theories have been put forward about the author's life, family and friends, his motive in writing the novel,

A still of the Yueju opera *Dream of the Red Mansions*

A painting of the Grand View Garden

the merits and demerits of the different editions, and the true meaning of the novel, etc. Even many details of the story have been explained in different ways by scholars. Today an increasing number of literary critics in foreign countries are joining in the study of the book. The novel has been translated into several other languages. Two English versions are very popular.

Perhaps no other novel, Chinese or foreign, has been enjoyed and discussed by so many people for so long a time. This fact proves the greatness of the novel and the unique position it has in the long history of Chinese literature.

23

Traditional Chinese Painting

In ancient times, painting was done mainly for practical purposes, such as decorations for clothing, buildings, furniture and utensils. There were also paintings on superstitious articles. Some of those earliest works were beautiful and interesting enough to evoke the admiration of people of today, especially archaeologists. The painters' names were of course never known, for they were not professional artists, but craftsmen.

The first painter mentioned in historical works was perhaps Mao Yanshou, who was ordered by an emperor of the Western Han to paint portraits of the women in the palace. This event of about 2,000 years ago showed that figure painting started very early in China.

Admonitions to the Court Ladies (part), by Gu Kaizhi of the Eastern Jin Dynasty

During the Han, Wei and Jin dynasties, many names of the painters and their paintings were recorded in various books, but none of their works were extant today except one by Gu Kaizhi (348–409) of the Eastern Jin. Gu was an official-scholar born in Wuxi, Jiangsu, said to be good at painting many things, including figures. He painted a handscroll (a long horizontal painting rolled up to be unrolled when viewed) called *Admonitions to the Court Ladies*, in which there were several persons, all vividly done. It was one of the rare objects owned by the Qing royal faimly. In the war of 1900, when Western armies invaded Beijing, it was seized by the British troops, and today it is in the British Museum in London. This painting is the earliest one that can be found today.

In the period of the Southern and Northern Dynasties, as Buddhism was widely spread in North and South China. Buddhist sculpture and painting flourished in many places. In Yungang near Datong, Shanxi, and Longmen near Luoyang, Henan, a series of caves were built with hundreds of stone images of Buddhist gods carved in them. They are all excellent sculptures. As for Buddhist painting, the largest treasure house was in Dunhuang, Gansu.

For several hundred years, from the 4th to the 10th centuries, believers in Buddhism built grottoes in Dunhuang, and in each grotto they painted beautiful pictures of Buddhist gods and scenes from Buddhist scriptures and stories. Today there are still 492 grottoes with about 45,000 square meters of paintings in them. In addition, there are over 2,000 colorful clay sculptures. Known all over the world, the grottoes attract hundreds of visitors daily from other places in China and other countries. The paintings and the manuscripts and books discovered in those grottoes are most valuable as relics of Chinese culture. They have been studied by scholars not only of China, but of many other countries.

In those early periods, landscapes were also painted, but they mainly served as the backgrounds of figures. It was in the Sui and Tang times that landscape painting gradually became independent. Wu Daoxuan, also called Wu Daozi, and Li Sixun, both Tang painters, were once asked by the reigning emperor to paint the

A Dunhuang fresco

scenery of the Jialing River in Sichuan. Li spent one whole month on the work, while Wu used only one day. Li's painting was rich in details, and Wu's was free and imaginative. Later, the famous poet Wang Wei, who was also a good painter, painted all kinds of things, including landscapes. Of his achievement, Su Shi, the great Song poet, said that there was painting in Wang Wei's poetry, and there was poetry in his painting.

Some painters of the period of the Five Dynasties and Ten States (907–979) were especially good at painting flowers and birds. During the Song Dynasty that followed, landscapes and flowers and birds were more popular than figures among artists, who tended to think that landscapes, flowers and birds were of greater aesthetic value. Therefore there were three main themes in painting: figures, landscapes, and flowers and birds. In addition, there was Buddhist art.

In the Song, Yuan, Ming and Qing periods, landscape painting was far more important than the other categories. This had something to do with the part played by the scholar-officials,

Riverside Scene on Qingming Festival (part), by Zhang Zeduan of the Northern Song Dynasty

or literary men, who took painting as their pastime or means of expressing their vision and personality. In painting landscapes, they did not try to reproduce faithfully what they saw in nature. Instead, they often altered the real scenery or highlighted some aspects of it to reveal their emotions or aspirations.

In such landscapes, human beings are usually not an important part. They are seldom in the foreground or in the center. If there were human beings in a painting, they were generally very small in contrast with huge mountains and rivers. They stand or sit among trees or rocks, gazing at and admiring distant mountains or waterfalls. They are in perfect harmony with nature, or rather they have become part of nature. This perhaps shows the influence of Taoist philosophy on those scholar-official painters.

Some literary men enjoyed painting plums, orchids, bamboo

and chrysanthemums. To these painters the four plants were especially elegant and had no vulgar taste. Moreover, they thought these plants were symbolic of certain moral qualities. The plum blossomed before other flowers, in cold winter or early spring, and the chrysanthemum in late autumn disregarding frost. They had their pride and persevering spirit. The bamboo was upright; and the orchid pure.

Before the Tang, most painters were professionals, or people whose main work was painting. They commonly aimed at reproducing the fine details of the things they painted. But after the Tang many literary men also painted. Their style was different. To them ideas were more important than the real appearance of objects. They painted ideas. So they painted with greater freedom than professionals.

Traditional Chinese painters draw pictures mainly with lines, and often in one color—black. The brushes they used were made of the hair of animals, including rabbit, sheep, goat and wolf. Black ink came from solid sticks made of pine soot and glue. Paper and silk were the usual painting surfaces. In short, the tools for painting were exactly the same as those for handwriting.

Color was of secondary importance. In one colored painting there was often one prominent color to highlight its main part, and there might be other vague colors to strengthen the effect.

There were different formats. The hand scroll had a long, horizontal form. It was suited to long and narrow paintings, like that of the scenery of a river or scenes of a city. *Riverside Scene on Qingming Festival*, done in the Northern Song period, presented the scenes of a busy street with bridges, shops, houses and hundreds of people, was perhaps the longest and best-known painting of this type.

The hanging scroll was more common. It was long and vertical, with various sizes. At its bottom there was a wooden cylinder to provide weight when the painting was hung, and make the rolling easy when it was stored.

Fans, either round or oval ones made of silk, or foldable ones made of paper, were often painted by artists, who had to suit their compositions to the fixed shapes.

One unique feature of traditional

A hanging scroll

Paintings on fans

Chinese painting was the inscription. When a painting was completed, the artist himself, or a friend of his, or it's a later owner, might write comments on the work, usually interpretations of its theme or significance, in beautiful handwriting. Such comments were often written in verse. They made the work enjoyable in three ways: as a painting, as a literary work, and as a calligraphic achievement.

Then there was the artist's personal seal, which was imprinted in special red paste on the painting below his name. Although a seal contained only the two or three characters of a person's name, its design and the way the characters were written were infinitely varied. A well-designed seal was a small precious work of art. Many painters

A seal

were also good at designing and carving seals. So the traditional Chinese artist might be a master of four arts: painting, calligraphy, poetry and seal making.

24

The Opium War and Changes in Cultural Trends After It

In 1840 Britain attacked China for a criminal purpose—to protect the opium trade.

In the early 19th century, the British East India Company smuggled to China large quantities of opium produced in India, which was then a British colony. This illegal trade not only cost China enormous sums of money, but did great harm to the health and moral quality of those who were addicted to the drug. So clear-headed officials in the Qing government like Lin Zexu wanted to have the trade completely banned. The Qing rulers also saw the danger of the spread of opium, and in 1838 appointed Lin High Commissioner and entrusted him with the task of banning the opium trade in Guangzhou, where most British opium dealers were staying and doing business.

Opium   Opium pipes

After arriving in Guangzhou early in 1839, Lin took resolute and strict measures to ban the trade. He compelled the British merchants to surrender all their opium, totaling 22,000 chests (one chest containing about 60 kg of opium) and had it publicly burned in Humen, not far from Guangzhou.

The British government, urged by the interest groups connected with the opium trade, decided to wage war on China. They sent a fleet of over 40 battleships with 4,000 troops to Chinese seas.

The invaders were repelled by the army and people of

Destruction of Opium at Humen

Guangdong, where Lin Zexu had made necessary preparations. The British fleet then sailed north and occupied Dinghai off the Zhejiang coast. After that they attacked several important but poorly defended coastal cities of Zhejiang, Jiangsu and Fujian. In Jiangsu they entered the Yangtze River and went as far west as Zhenjiang and Nanjing, thus cutting off transport between the South and the North. They had met with only weak resistance by troops of the Qing government, but in many places the people had fought bravely against and inflicted heavy losses on them. The decadent and corrupt Qing rulers were so frightened by the superior weapons of the British, and so afraid of the rise of the people, that they had wavered all along between fighting and suing for peace, and finally decided to accept the British demands so as to end the war. Lin Zexu was demoted and exiled to Xinjiang.

As a result of the war, the Treaty of Nanjing, the first unequal treaty imposed on China by a Western power, was signed on board a British battleship anchored near Nanjing in August 1842. The treaty stipulated that China should pay Britain an indemnity of 21,000,000 silver dollars, cede Hong Kong to

Britain, open five ports (Guangzhou, Xiamen, Fuzhou, Ningbo and Shanghai) to foreign trade, and tariffs on British goods should be fixed by mutual agreement. In the next year Britain forced on China two new agreements, which allowed British consuls to try British people who had committed crimes in China according to British law, and made China give Britain all the privileges in trade China would give to any other country. In other words, China gave Britain the right of consular jurisdiction and unilateral most-favored-nation treatment.

China's defeat in the Opium War exposed her military weakness and political backwardness. Western powers saw that it was easy to force her to accept unequal conditions. So after the war Britain and other Western countries, including France, Germany, Russia and the United States, and Japan in the east, jointly or separately started aggressive wars on China, or bullied China in different ways, to demand privileges, special rights, indemnities, concessions and even territory, and generally they got what they wanted. Chinese history in the second half of the 19th century was full of such humiliating events. They marked the turn of China from a feudal country into a semi-colonial and semi-feudal country.

This situation awakened patriotic Chinese to the necessity of finding out the causes of China's weakness and ways of rejuvenating the country. Scholars with advanced ideas like Lin Zexu and Wei Yuan considered it important to understand the history and geography of Western countries, and learn from their strong points. Lin compiled a book called *Knowledge of the Four Continents*, and Wei expanded its content and compiled a big book called *Illustrated Records of Maritime Countries*. Wei said that China should "learn the advanced techniques of foreign countries in order to control them."

Many government officials believed that China was weak mainly because her military equipment was backward. Western troops had rifles and cannons, while Chinese soldiers were armed only with swords and spears. Therefore these officials, Zeng Guofan and Li Hongzhang among them, began to build factories producing weapons. To facilitate production, mines and factories making steel and other materials were

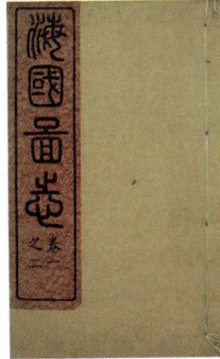

Illustrated Records of Maritime Countries

also set up. The Qing government bought several battleships from foreign countries, intending to build a navy. Groups of students were sent to Europe and Japan to study science and technology. This development was later called the Westernization Drive.

In 1894 Japan invaded Korea and Chinese territory Taiwan. The Qing troops sent to help defend Korea were defeated. The new Chinese navy, after fighting the Japanese navy courageously on the Yellow Sea, was almost completely destroyed in its harbor Weihaiwei by the Japanese troops landed on Shandong. The Qing rulers who did not want to continue to fight were forced to accept all Japanese demands, including the cession of Taiwan to Japan. The outcome of the war made it clear that westernization alone could not turn China into a strong country, because the rulers who made policies and directed wars were weak and decadent.

After the war of 1894 China was in a deep national crisis, for the big powers threatened to partition China. Scholars who were worried about the fate of the country called for reform, not only in industry and military affairs, but also in the political system.

Outstanding among these people were Kang Youwei, Liang Qichao, Yan Fu and Tan Sitong.

Kang and over 1,300 other scholars who had gathered in Beijing for the final stage of the imperial examinations submitted a memorial to Emperor Guangxu suggesting political reform. Kang was for the substitution of constitutional monarchy for feudal autocracy. Liang, once a student of Kang's, helped Kang by writing articles propagating reformist ideas. Yan studied in England for a few years, and after returning to China devoted his time to translating English philosophical, political and economic classics, such as Huxley's *Evolution and Ethics*. Tan was more radical than the others. He wrote *On Benevolence* criticizing traditional ideas.

The reformists frequently made speeches, published books and wrote articles in newspapers to explain the necessity of reform. They were in a way helped by the critical situation of the country, which showed that China had no way out except reform. But conservatives, or diehards, were still a strong force in the

China Merchants Steam Navigation Company in Shanghai

Kang Youwei

Liang Qichao

Tan Sitong

country, especially in the ruling class. They were against all changes. "The way handed down from ancestors should never be changed." they said, and they contended what was necessary was to change men, not law, for all faults came from men's wrong thinking.

In the fierce debate between the two sides, the conservatives usually quoted from Confucius, Mencius and other ancient philosophers, and the reformists often gave new interpretations to some classics. They even tried to prove that Confucius also favored changes. Moreover, they made use of new learning like the philosophy of evolution to show that change was a principle that governed all things. To a certain extent this debate prepared public opinion for the coming reform.

In 1898 Kang Youwei submitted to the emperor another memorial, in which he warned that only political changes could save the country, and that the country would perish without major changes. He had always hoped that the emperor would start reform from above, and had never thought of calling on the people to demand reform from below.

This time Emperor Guangxu was impressed by and agreed to Kang's views and suggestions. In June 1898 he gave Kang and a

Portrait of Empress Dowager Cixi   Portrait of Emperor Guangxu

few other reformists important positions in the government and empowered them to carry out reform.

They took mainly economic and educational measures, such as the encouragement of industry and commerce, the establishment of schools, the reform of the imperial examination system, and the abolition of some unnecessary government organs. They never suggested organizing a parliament. But the conservative force led by Empress Dowager Cixi, who had real power, bitterly hated and strongly opposed these measures. With the help of some military men, Cixi counterattacked in June. She put Emperor Guangxu under house arrest, and killed Tan Sitong and five other reformists. Kang Youwei and Liang Qichao narrowly escaped. The hundred-day reform was thus brought to an end.

The failure of the reformists taught some progressive people a lesson: it would be impossible to change the political system under Qing rule. Shortly afterwards, people with more radical ideas led by Dr. Sun Yatsen began preparing for armed uprisings to overthrow the Qing Dynasty. After a series of failures, they finally succeeded in 1911.

25

Causes of the Long Feudal Period

From the earliest times down to the middle of the 19th century, Chinese society went through three stages: primitive society, slave society, and feudal society. The Xia Dynasty ruled over a slave society. In the Shang period there was definitely a slave system, as inscriptions on oracle bones showed how slaves were used and ill-treated. During the Western Zhou (1046–771 BC) or Eastern Zhou (770–256 BC) Chinese society entered the feudal stage. This social system was to last more than 2,500 years until it was shaken by foreign cannons during the Opium War.

During this long period, there were many changes in dynasties; there were many large-scale wars and many peasant uprisings; and for a long time China was under the rule of minority groups. But the social system remained unchanged—it was essentially feudal though seeds of capitalism did appear.

Compared with Europe, where feudalism lasted about 1,000 years, China had a much longer feudal period. Many causes have been mentioned. Among them are the following:

1. A predominant natural economy. This was the economic foundation of the feudal system. Throughout the country the

peasants, who made up over 90 percent of the population, produced and made nearly everything for themselves, and not for the market. They grew rice or wheat or corn, and they also raised pigs, goats and chickens, and grew vegetables. They grew cotton and hemp, and wove very coarse cloth with their handlooms. They made their own tools, furniture and other things they used. In short, there were very few things that they had to buy from shops in town. Even if they wanted to buy something, in most cases they had no money, because they had very few things that they could sell.

The landlords were rich enough to buy things, but as they made up a very small portion of the population, they could not consume much. And it was not their habit to invest their money in production. They squandered their money, bought more land with their money, or left their money to their children.

As a result, the market for industrial products was limited, and so was the source of capital. These limitations made it difficult for industry (or handicrafts) and commerce to develop quickly. It followed that the industrial producers and merchants were weak both economically and politically. They were closely linked to or controlled by the landlords.

Besides, the rulers of most dynasties considered agriculture more important than industry or commerce, and made policies favorable to landlords and unfavorable to merchants.

These factors slowed down the growth of capitalism and kept feudalism going.

2. A stable feudal political system. For about 2,000 years from the Qin Dynasty to the end of the Qing Dynasty, the country was governed more or less in the same way. There were modifications from dynasty to dynasty in the organization and

workings of the government, but there were very few fundamental changes in the main structure of the political system. All powers were in the hands of the emperor alone, who was assisted by a group of ministers led by the prime minister. Local governors were appointed by the central government. The common people had no democratic rights at all. No official was elected and no organ in the government represented them. But the people's interests were taken into consideration in two ways, though indirectly. One was the system of supervision. There were high-ranking officials whose duty was to inspect and examine the work and conduct of all administrators and punish those who had abused their powers. The other was the imperial examination system. Scholars who had passed certain examinations were given government posts, and some of them understood the problems and wishes of the people.

In spite of its undemocratic nature and many faults, this political system seemed to suit the social conditions on the whole. Except when there were wars or great political upheavals, the country was effectively governed and law and order were maintained.

3. A highly-developed feudal culture. Chinese culture was highly developed in the feudal period. It played an important part in keeping the country unified, though it had such a large area and such a huge size of population; in maintaining the continuity of Chinese history. During the period of Southern and Northern Dynasties and the Yuan and Qing, China was partly or wholly under the rule of national minorities for about 600 years. Invariably the military conquerors were conquered by Chinese culture. They learned to rule China in the Chinese way and accepted Chinese culture. This fact showed that advanced Chinese

Temple of Confucius, Beijing

culture was more powerful than military or political forces.

The core of Chinese culture was Confucianism. It was made the state thought in the Western Han. After that most scholars, officials, and even emperors, professed to follow it, and some truthfully followed it, in their conduct and work. As Confucianism laid special emphasis on moral principles, humane government and education, its influence was mainly positive. It also stressed the importance of loyalty to the ruler and filial piety to one's parents. These ideas were helpful to the stability of feudal rule. Confucianism valued ancient traditions, such as the institutions of the Western Zhou, and gave great respect to ancient sages like King Yao, King Shun, King Yu, King Wen, King Wu and the Duke of Zhou, taking their rule as the model for all ages. In other words, it taught people to look backwards. This may have fostered the conservative tendency of the Chinese people.

Besides Confucianism there were two other influential philosophies: Taoism and Buddhism. Taoism advocated an escape from social duties, and the enjoyment of freedom, quietude and peace. This attitude could do no harm to feudal rule. Buddhism

Qingyang Palace, Chengdu, Sichuan Province

urged people to be passive, to give up all desires, to do good things so that they might have a better lot in their next lives. This doctrine could only make its believers obedient and tolerant, instead of fighting against oppression and exploitation.

It is clear that Chinese culture of the feudal period, especially Confucianism, gave moral guidance and support to the feudal system. It made China one of the most advanced countries in the world for nearly 2,000 years, but it hindered social change or progress during the last stage of the period.

These economic, political and cultural factors combined to make the feudal period last so long in China. There were of course other factors. One of them was China's lack of contact with the outside world. There was some foreign influence on Chinese culture. Buddhism, for instance, came from India. But foreign influence never changed the character of Chinese culture. Chinese society and culture developed along their own path until the outbreak of the Opium War in 1840.

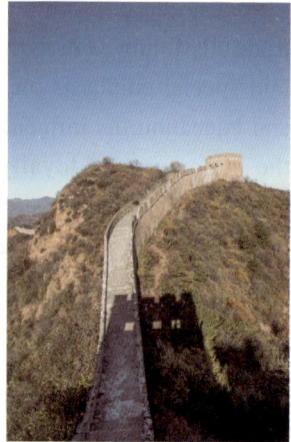